THE COUNTRY STORE

THE COUNTRY STORE

Traditional Food ✻ Country Crafts ✻ Natural Decorations

STEPHANIE DONALDSON

PHOTOGRAPHS BY MICHELLE GARRETT

LORENZ BOOKS

NEW YORK • LONDON • SYDNEY • BATH

To Ann – a consistently creative cook and valued friend

This edition published in 1996 by Lorenz Books
an imprint of Anness Publishing Inc.
administrative office: 27 West 20th Street, New York, NY 10011

© 1996 Anness Publishing Limited

Lorenz Books are available for bulk purchase for sales promotion and for premium use. For details write or call the manager of special sales, LORENZ BOOKS, 27 West 20th Street, New York, NY 10011; (212) 807-6739

Produced by Anness Publishing Limited
1 Boundary Row
London SE1 8HP

ISBN 1 85967 257 4

A CIP catalogue record is available from the British Library

Publisher: Joanna Lorenz
Editorial Manager: Helen Sudell
Designer: Lisa Tai
Photographer: Michelle Garrett

Printed and bound in Hong Kong

Picture credits: Bridgeman Art Library, London: p12 *Preparing for Dinner* by Frederick Daniel Hardy, Wolverhampton Art Gallery; p13 *Preserving Jam* by Frederick Daniel Hardy, Bourne Gallery, Reigate.

Contents

Introduction

The history and traditions of the country store. How to prepare, stock, use and display provisions.

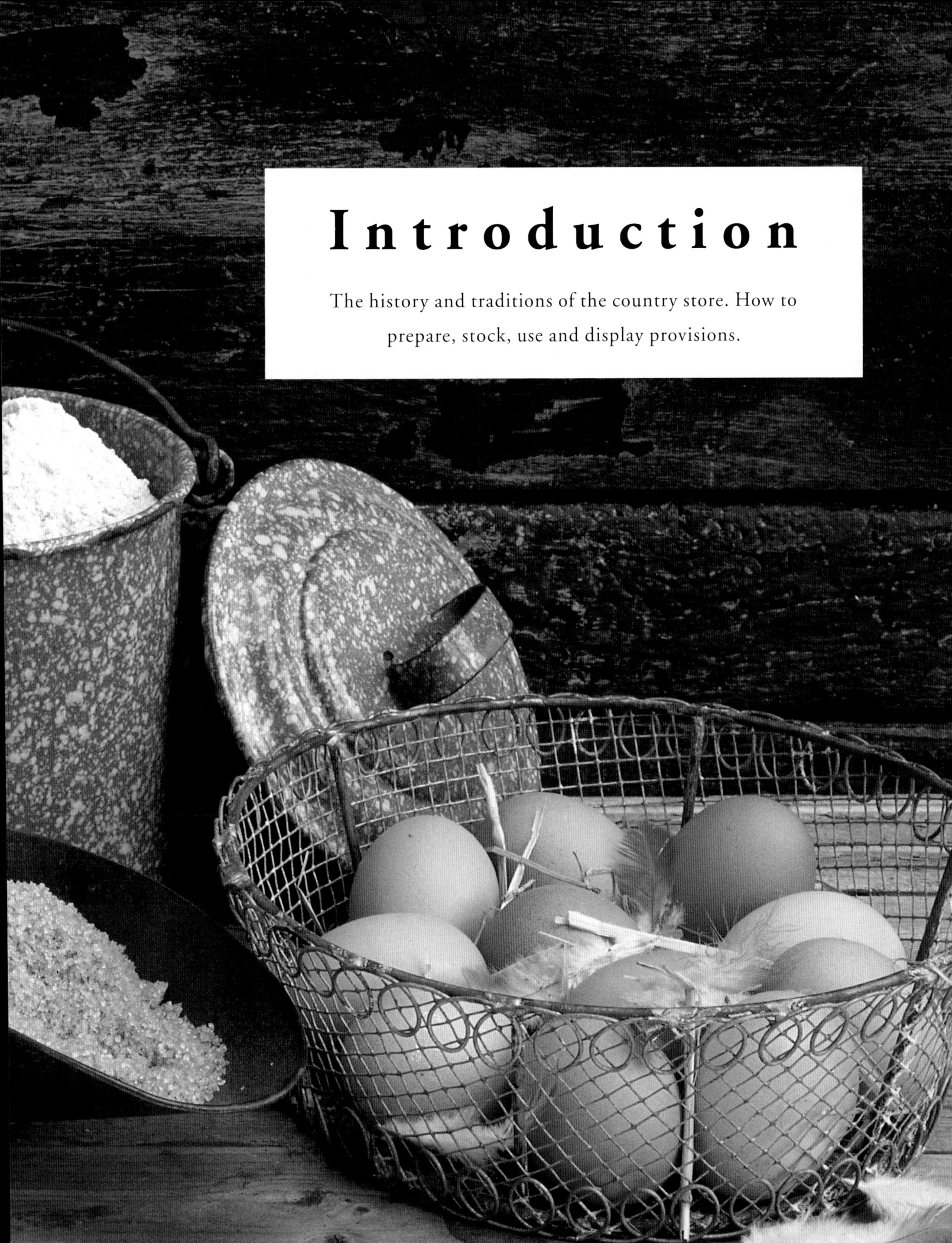

A simpler way of life

Our constant search for progress has resulted in a world where, for many of us, the seasons have become largely irrelevant, except as a backdrop for a change of clothing and sporting activities. We can eat fresh cherries from Chile in January, avocados from Israel throughout the year and, like spoiled children, indulge our every culinary whim regardless of the time of year. The price we pay for this progress is not just the cost of these unseasonal foods, but it is also an alienation from our deepest instincts to sow and reap and store, to mark the change of the seasons in festivals and thanksgiving and to pass on the knowledge of these things to future generations.

There is still a hunger in us for these old ways, and although few of us regret the advent of many of modern life's labor-saving devices and comforts, we are drawn to the simplicity of earlier times, when survival was a reward rather than an expectation. Although we no longer need to follow the progress of the seasons to ensure our survival, we can still participate in seasonal activities and will find our lives immeasurably enriched by doing so.

The sowing of seeds, even if it is just a pot of parsley on the windowsill, is the beginning of a relationship with the plants that germinate, the picking of apples from the garden follows the beauty of the spring blossom and the slow growth of the tiny green fruit to their full-flushed maturity when we can enjoy the satisfaction of our own harvest.

I hope very much that *The Country Store* will inspire you to take some time out of our busy and hectic modern life to experience for yourself the pleasure of the seasons: to discover the enjoyment to be had in baking, pickling and preserving; to try the simple natural remedies and fragrant beauty products and potpourris; and to celebrate the progress of the year with seasonal decorations and foods.

Right: *An assortment of invaluable items to collect for your projects: blocks of beeswax, candles, flower waters, essential oils, dried herbs and flower heads.*

A brief history of the pantry

In the Middle Ages, the monasteries were the repositories of knowledge, and high ranking amongst the monks was the cellarer who had overall responsibility for providing the religious community with all the food and drink that was needed throughout the year. He was an expert in the growing, harvesting and preserving of large quantities of food, and while life in general was short and not very sweet, the religious orders were well nourished and far healthier than the general population. The cellarer's knowledge of herbs and spices, of salts, vinegars and oils increased as new plants and flavorings were introduced from other lands, and his uses of them, as well as his observations, were meticulously recorded in what were the forebears of our modern recipe books.

In Elizabethan England it became customary for gentlewomen to write down the secrets of their household management in a book to pass on their skills from one generation to the next. As well as recipes, this book would include simple remedies, lotions and potions, potpourris and polishes, many of which we would recognize and even keep in our pantry today.

As the ability to read and write spread among the population, this tradition was taken up more generally, and for generations families and friends passed on and exchanged family recipes to keep the pantry full. It was not until Victorian times, and the advent of tomes such as Mrs Beeton's *Book of Household Management*, that this knowledge passed from the family into the hands of "experts" and began to acquire a mystique that removed it from its place as a common part of our everyday lives.

Above: *In the past, salt was of great social and economic importance and was an extremely valuable commodity.*

Left: *In former times, all but the poorest households would have owned a cow, and the dairy was as important as the still room to the countrywoman.*

Right: *Blue and white enamelware is enduringly popular, and is appreciated for its durability, practicality and simple design.*

Traditions, folklore and fact

In the days when good husbandry was an essential skill for every country dweller, the circle of the seasons entailed an endless progression of tasks that had to be completed to ensure the fertility and productivity of the land followed by a fruitful harvest that would see the family through the long winter. Everyone had their tasks: even the smallest of the children would be put to work picking stones, scaring the birds and gathering fruit and vegetables. As the daughters grew up they would learn the skills of the kitchen, the dairy and still room from their mother, and by the time they left to make their own homes, they would be accomplished in all the necessary tasks of everyday life. For everyone, such important festivals as Easter, Harvest Festival, Thanksgiving and Christmas were markers in the year, and these celebrations were rewards for the hard work of daily life as well as religious occasions.

Many folk tales and traditional rhymes were originally devised as a reminder of the seasonal tasks. In Tudor England, for example, the poet and writer Thomas Tusser was particularly free with his advice, instructing farmer and housewife alike in books with edifying titles

Below: *Preparing food for the table was a very time-consuming task. Vegetables had to be picked from the garden, scrubbed clean and then peeled before being chopped up for the pot.*

such as *Five Hundred Points of Good Husbandry* and *Housewifely Admonitions*. A typical example of his rhyming recommendations is this little verse on the efficacy of wormwood to prevent the infestation of houses by fleas:

While wormwood hath seed, get a bundle or twain,
to save against March, to make flea to refrain:
Where chamber is swept, and wormwood is strown,
no flea, for his life, dare abide to be known.

In other words, wormwood should be picked when it has gone to seed in the late summer or the fall, hung up to dry over winter and then used at the time of spring-cleaning in early spring when it will be most effective against fleas. In an age when books were a luxury, such rhymes made it easier to remember advice and knowledge.

Above: *Making jams and preserves would have been an activity that the whole family joined in on, from collecting fruits from the bushes around the house or farm to helping Mother with the cooking – and eating – of the produce.*

Although superstition and folklore certainly played their part in rural life, country people have always been, by and large, great realists and were far too busy working to spend much time on spells and potions. These were largely the province of doctors and charlatans whose cures were frequently more dangerous than the illnesses themselves. Country people preferred to rely on simple remedies that every housewife prepared in her pantry. Just as we once again appreciate the quality of homemade preserves, so we are also acknowledging that many of the old remedies were based on understanding rather than superstition.

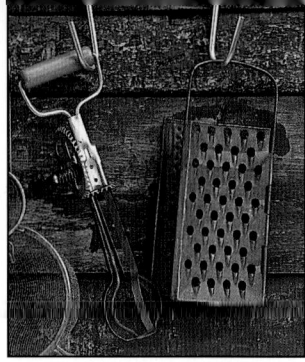

Stocking up

It is quite possible to make practically everything shown in this book without having to buy any special equipment, but the projects will be easier to do if you have a good range of basic kitchen equipment. The following items are recommended:

• a large, heavy-based pan for preserving and sterilizing
• a good selection of clean glass jars and bottles
• fresh rubber seals for preserving jars
• accurate scales
• measuring jugs
• a selection of mixing bowls
• a *bain-marie* or double boiler – if you are also going to make cosmetics, you will need a second bowl to fit your saucepan, which you should keep purely for this purpose. Also keep a set of the following utensils for cosmetics only:
• metal whisk
• wooden spoon
• set of measuring spoons

BASIC MATERIALS AND INGREDIENTS

If you are fortunate enough to live in the country, you may already have a productive garden and access to fruitful orchards and woods to provide many of the basic materials you will use as you begin to fill your country pantry, but for those of us less blessed, there is still the pleasure of making, even if we do not do the growing and the gathering ourselves. The best farm stands are a good source of freshly picked fruit and vegetables, as are farms where you can pick your own produce. Even city dwellers will find many bargains at their local market, especially at the end of the day, when a whole box can be bought at a considerable discount. An elderly neighbor whose garden is becoming neglected may welcome your planting a vegetable patch and sharing the produce with them. And in a plentiful year, a friend with an apple tree will think you are doing him a favor if you ask for some fruit.

Everyone should grow some herbs. They give our food savor, stimulate the appetite, can benefit health and make a fragrant addition to the home. Herbs are widely used in the projects in this book, and whatever the scale of your herb garden – a windowsill or a formal garden – you will be able to use everything you grow.

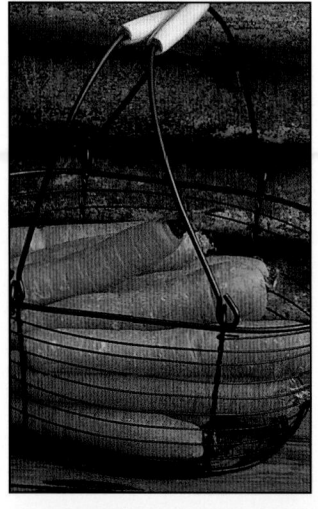

Left: *Use a wire basket for picking produce; excess soil can drop through the base and good air circulation keeps the vegetables in prime condition for several days.*

Below: *Fresh ingredients, whether home-grown or store-bought, are the starting point and inspiration for everything you will make to fill your pantry.*

Above: *There is an intrinsic beauty to old, well-used kitchen utensils and equipment, and provided they do the job and can be properly cleaned, there is no need to replace them.*

Right: *Cox's Orange Pippin apples may not have the glossy perfection of some other varieties, but their flavor is unsurpassed.*

Whether you are collecting ingredients for cooking, for natural remedies, for fragrance or celebration, it is vitally important that they are always of the highest possible quality. For example, for bottling, fully ripe but firm fruit will give the best flavor. Herbs are at their most potent just before they flower. Vegetables should be used as soon as possible after they have been picked or bought. Essential oils should always be purchased from a reputable supplier, and dried flowers should be from the most recent harvest. In other words, quite simply, if your intention is to make a quality product, you must use only quality ingredients.

Growing and gathering for storage

One of the great advantages of growing your own produce is that you know precisely what has been used on the plants: no over-enthusiastic applications of fertilizers or other chemicals. Ideally, just the sweat of your brow and lots of compost. If possible grow your vegetables, fruit and herbs organically because they will be better for you and organic cultivation is also better for the health of the soil. If you do need to control pests, try to use natural predators wherever possible. They are increasingly available and as effective as chemical sprays when used correctly.

PURCHASING

Organically grown foods are also available from specialist food stores and some supermarkets. While they do not always have the glossy perfection of their chemically stimulated relatives, their flavor is generally excellent. Remember that what you wish to preserve in your country store is flavor and fragrance, so it is important to choose varieties that have these attributes; a visually perfect and glowing red apple that has the texture of cotton balls will not taste any better once it has been bottled.

GATHERING

Fortunately, it is now easier to collect fruits, berries and nuts from the bushes, as the days when farmers and highway maintenance teams sprayed our roadsides with weed killers are mostly past. There is a welcome return of a profusion of wild flowers that make field edges so lovely in the spring and summer months and a corresponding burgeoning of bushes abundant with elderflowers, blackberries and rose hips. When gathering from the wild, always do so respectfully. Always make sure that you leave plenty for the wildlife, since plants are an important food source for them, and also something for others who would like to share in nature's bounty. Never pick an endangered species. It is your responsibility to find out which plants are protected in your area and it is important that you do so; your local council or library will be able to help you.

Anyone who has gathered blackberries, blueberries or wild strawberries will tell you that it takes a surprisingly long time to collect a usable quantity, and it always seems that the best and most plenteous fruit is just out of reach. So make gathering a group activity, preferably with people of varying heights and also a hooked stick to reach those elusive high branches. What can be a chore for an individual can be fun for the whole family, who will also benefit from the fresh air and exercise.

Right: *Home-grown peas have an unrivaled flavor and shelling them while sitting in the sunshine is a restful occupation.*

Above: *Sow small quantities of seeds frequently, in order to provide a succession of produce throughout the season.*

Above: *Beet thinnings provide delicious baby beets and the leaves can be cooked just like spinach.*

Right: *Gather your herbs in the morning, when they are at their most aromatic. Be sure to pick regularly.*

HARVESTING

This is the time when your efforts are rewarded, when those carefully nurtured fruits, vegetables, blossoms and herbs are gathered in ready to be used to fill your store. Choose your harvest time carefully; a dry sunny day with a light breeze is ideal – for you and the produce. Flowers and herbs should be gathered only after the dew has dried but before midday. You must pick fruit carefully to avoid bruising or damaging it in any way. Young vegetables should be gathered in small batches for immediate use, and mature root vegetables lifted before the first frosts.

Using and showing off your creations

There is a temptation to treat the contents of the pantry rather like works of art, treasures to be displayed and admired but never touched. But then you miss out on the best part of having a pantry – the consumption. Once you have tasted and enjoyed the fruits of your labors, it becomes easier to accept that your pantry is an ever-changing Aladdin's cave of treats and temptations rather than an end in itself.

If considerations of space, time and money permit it, then a cool, dark closet or cellar is the perfect place to keep jams, pickles and preserves, but failing that, set aside a cabinet in your kitchen for storing homemade goods. Warm, light rooms are not ideal for the storage of preserves or for drying flowers and herbs, but if you dry some flowers and herbs especially for display and have a pretty shelf where you can show off your preserves for a little while before you use them, then you can keep the majority of your creations in good condition and not miss out on the compliments.

Above: *Miniature galvanized buckets make attractive containers for a collection of medicinal herbs and flowers.*

Left: *Turn your fresh herbs into an attractive feature in a room by storing them in pretty glass containers.*

Right: *Autumn leaves and bows made out of raffia or coarse string can give your jars of preserves an attractive rustic finish.*

Decorating and presenting

The finishing touches can turn an everyday item into something special. A simple pot of jam, for instance, becomes a special gift when it is presented in a pretty jar with the lid covered by a beautiful autumn leaf tied on with raffia. And a bottle of aromatic chili oil does not need a written label to identify its flavorings when its neck is decorated with a bunch of chilis.

Colorful confections are all the more tempting when individually wrapped in cellophane and tied with a raffia bow, or when nestling inside a decorative wooden box.

Celebration wines and ratafias become sublime when bottled in decorative glass bottles and adorned with gilded leaves and corks.

Above: *A decorative touch turns this lemon- and lime-flavored vinegar into a perfect gift.*

Above: *Natural materials make inexpensive packaging.*

Left: *A dried orange slice tied around a jar of marmalade is an unusual but eloquent label.*

Right: *The autumnal colors of the potpourri are echoed in the matte brown ribbon and the sisal string used to decorate the cellophane bag.*

The Kitchen

An irresistible collection of preserves and pickles, flavored oils
and vinegars, baked goods and sweet gifts.

Fruit and vegetables

Whether the fruit and vegetables you use are from your own garden or somewhere else, produce that is destined for preserving should always be of the best possible quality. When growing your own produce, choose the varieties whose good flavor is particularly mentioned. It is amazing how many modern varieties that are grown for disease resistance and reliability seem to have totally sacrificed flavor in the search for the standardization of color and size. Therefore, if you are buying fruit and vegetables, it is always a good idea to taste them before you start preserving, just to make sure that they have a flavor that is worth keeping. Less than perfect fruit can be used in the making of jellies, chutneys, and the like, but because they deteriorate quickly, you should be ready for action as soon as you have collected them.

Wherever possible, store your fruit and vegetables in a dark, cool but frost-free place with good ventilation. They will keep extremely well under these conditions, especially if they are prepared for storage beforehand. Mature root vegetables such as carrots, parsnips and beets will keep for months when stored in boxes of sand (make sure you keep them in horticultural, not builder's, sand). Apples and pears can be kept on slatted wooden shelves, if they are not touching, or you can wrap them individually in paper and store them in boxes. They should last through the winter, especially if the varieties stored are good keepers.

Never store fruit near potatoes because it will become tainted. It is important to check your stored fruit and vegetables regularly, using the fruit as it ripens and removing any pieces that show signs of rot, which can spread quickly to the good fruit.

Below: *The flavor of tomatoes is improved by storing them at room temperature rather than in a refrigerator. Ideally, tomatoes should not be picked until they are fully ripe, but even an underripe fruit will improve if you store it this way.*

Above: *In the fall, prepare unblemished apples for storage during the winter. Each fruit should be wrapped in newspaper and stored on a wooden tray or in a cardboard box. Alternatively, store them unwrapped and not touching on slatted wooden shelves.*

Right: *The traditional way of storing mature root vegetables is to arrange them in layers in silver sand. Then cover them completely and store in a cool, dark place and they will keep for months, retaining a good flavor and texture.*

Herbs and flowers

If you have enough space in your garden, devoting a corner to the growing of herbs and flowers for drying will save you a great deal of money.

Herbs vary enormously in their aromatic strength and it is worth the time and expense to find a reputable herb grower who can sell you recommended named varieties of the herbs. If you do not have space to grow all the herbs you will need, there are companies that sell good-quality fresh and dried herbs by mail order far more cheaply than you can buy them at a supermarket. It is also worthwhile to visit shops that cater to Indian and Southeast Asian communities as a source of high-quality herbs and spices.

Herbs should be harvested before they have flowered, on a dry morning when the volatile oils will be at their most concentrated. From noon on, the oils start to evaporate into the surrounding air and flavor and fragrance are diminished.

Although herbs look very decorative when hung in open bunches from an old-fashioned clothes dryer, this is not the best way to dry them. Rather, the bunches of herbs should be rolled up in cones of brown paper, which will protect them from the light, then hung up to dry. Once they are fully dry (usually about two weeks), they should be taken down, stripped from their stems and stored in colored glass bottles away from the light. This will ensure that when you come to use the herbs for cooking or fragrance, they will still be intensely aromatic.

When growing flowers for drying, it is worth concentrating on the varieties that are difficult to come by or expensive, such as peonies and roses. Unless you have limitless space, there is little point in growing huge quantities of statice and helichrysum which can be bought easily and inexpensively.

When picking flowers for drying, they should be in full bloom but not full blown or they will drop their petals. They are also best gathered in the morning of a dry day. Hang them upside down in bunches in a warm, preferably not too light position and leave them there until they are dry to the touch. Peonies need to be dry right

Left: *A simple but very effective method of preserving your fresh herbs is to place them in a jar with a tight-fitting lid that contains sea salt. The herbs will then remain just as fresh and full of flavor as the day they were picked, and they will also give a delicious and distinctive flavor to the salt.*

Above: *Fresh herbs should be picked early in the day to capture the full intensity of their flavor. Keep them cool indoors until you are ready to use them, and replace them as soon as they start to look limp and bedraggled.*

Left: *The best way to dry fresh flowers is to tie them in small, loose bundles and hang them upside-down in a well-ventilated room. Keep out of direct sun to retain their vibrant colors.*

into the center of the flower and, to achieve this, it is advisable to place them in a low oven for about four hours after they have air-dried. Once you are confident that your flowers are fully dry, pack them into boxes and store in a dry place until you wish to use them. It is important to store dried flowers in boxes in order to keep them free of dust and preserve their color.

When buying dried flowers, it is best to purchase them from the grower, as theirs will have been stored under the best possible conditions and will not have been handled many times that often happens to dried flowers before they reach your local shop. Bargain dried flowers are nearly always old stock from the harvest before last and are not worth buying as they are brittle and faded.

Preserving produce

Preserving and drying are time-honored methods for prolonging the life of fruit, vegetables, herbs and sometimes flowers.

PRESERVING

Food can be preserved by being bottled in a variety of natural preservatives. Vegetables and herbs may be preserved by being packed in salt or immersed in brine. They can also be kept in oil, or used in small amounts to flavor oil. Vegetables, fruit and herbs can be pickled in or used to flavor vinegar and lemon juice. Even sugar and honey can be used for preserving fruit, herbs and flowers or can be flavored by them. Fruit, herbs and flowers can also be preserved in alcohol or turned into wines and liqueurs.

DRYING

Vegetables, herbs, fruit and flowers can all be preserved by being air-dried or placed in an oven set at a low temperature.

PROCESSING JARS IN WATER

1 *Line the base of the processing pan with either a folded cloth or a wooden trivet.*

2 *Place the bottles in the pan and fold cloths around each one to keep them from touching one another.*

3 *Fill the pan with cold water so that the bottles are covered by at least 1in of water.*

4 *Once the processing is complete and the bottles have cooled, check the seals by loosening the clips and making sure that they stay intact.*

STERILIZING

To ensure that harmful bacteria are eliminated from fruit and vegetables bottled in brine, syrup or their own juices, it is necessary to sterilize the bottles in a water bath or in the oven. To sterilize in water, follow the step instructions on the facing page. Alternatively, rest the lids on the bottles but do not seal. Stand them on a baking sheet lined with newspaper and place in a very low oven, 250°F.

Above: *Whether dried, bottled in syrup or preserved in oil, homemade preserves possess a surprising but striking beauty.*

Remove and seal immediately. As the bottles cool, a vacuum forms inside to complete the seal. Always use clean, undamaged bottles with fresh seals, and test every seal by turning it upside down. Bottles with failed seals should be used immediately or refrigerated.

Choosing and preparing containers

Glass jars and bottles have been used for the majority of projects in this chapter. Glass is durable, versatile and decorative. Its great advantage over aluminum, earthenware, terra-cotta, tin and porcelain is that it reveals and enhances its contents. Modern recycled glass has many of the qualities of antique glass, such as flaws and colorings, and is inexpensive. Old-fashioned candy jars, preserving jars and jam jars can still be bought in junk shops and, providing that they can be properly cleaned, used to great effect. However, they must not be used for any bottling that requires sterilizing.

STERILIZING JARS

To sterilize jars in a dishwasher, use the hottest wash but without any detergent. However, if you do not own a dishwasher, you can sterilize in the following way. First, wash the jars in hot, soapy water and rinse thoroughly. Stand them the right way up on a wooden board (making sure that they are not touching each other) and place the board in a cold oven. Turn the oven to very low (225°F) and leave the jars in for 30 minutes. If they are not to be used immediately, cover with a clean cloth.

Above: *Old-fashioned glass bottles are full of character and very attractive. They may be used for projects where containers should be clean but not necessarily sterile.*

Above: *There is a variety of bottles and jars that are designed especially for preserving, and provided they are not damaged in any way, they can be reused. However, you should always use fresh seals.*

SEALS

The type and effectiveness of the seal required depend on the process used. Providing jam jars are thoroughly washed and dried before use, a circle of greaseproof paper and a paper cover are sufficient to keep the contents in good condition. Wines and liqueurs keep well in bottles sealed with new corks. Vinegars and oils can be sealed with either corks or screw tops, but bottled fruit and vegetables must be sealed with new rubber seals.

Ideally, all your preserves should be labeled with a description of the contents and the date they were made. Self-adhering labels may

Above: With glass containers a descriptive label is not always necessary, but it is a good idea to record the date the preserve was made so that you can eat your creations in rotation.

be attached to the surface of the bottle or jar. Alternatively, card, wooden or metal labels may be tied around the neck. Bear in mind that if you intend to store your preserves in a cellar or cabinet where conditions may be slightly damp and paper labels can fall off or quickly deteriorate, it would be a good idea to use something more durable, such as metal or wooden labels.

31

Flavored oils

A selection of flavored oils will bring the taste of high summer to your cooking all year round. All flavored oils are best used within three months.

GARLIC OIL

Use this delicious oil in dressings and to brush on fish, meat and vegetables. In addition, it can save the fussy task of cleaning the garlic press every time you flavor with garlic! Do not throw away the poached garlic cloves, which are removed from the oil before bottling: they are ambrosial when spread on fresh French bread or used as a relish on meat, fish or vegetables. Either use immediately or pack them into a glass jar, cover with oil and refrigerate to use within ten days.

Makes 3 cups

25 large plump garlic cloves
3¾ cups cold-pressed virgin
*   olive oil*

Above: *Flavored oils in bottles are good to look at as well as useful ingredients.*

1 Peel the garlic cloves.

2 Heat the oil to a gentle simmer in a small saucepan, then add the garlic cloves and poach them for approximately 25 minutes, until tender and translucent. Leave in the pan until cool.

3 Strain the garlic cloves from the oil, reserving them for another use. Pour the oil into a clean bottle and seal with a screw top or cork. Use within ten days.

CHILI OIL

In the south of France, pizzas are enlivened by drizzling chili oil over them. You can also use this oil for stir-frying vegetables or grilling. For a more robust flavor, add garlic, thyme and peppercorns to this oil.

Makes 2¼ cups

2¼ cups virgin olive oil
1 small fresh green chili
5 small fresh red chilis

Fill a clean, dry bottle with the olive oil. Slice the green chili into thin rings and add them along with the whole red chilis to the olive oil.

   Cork tightly with a new cork and leave to infuse for 10–14 days. Shake the bottle occasionally during this time.

SAFFRON OIL

Saffron has never been surpassed as a flavoring. By weight it is certainly among the most expensive of all spices, but a little saffron goes a long way, especially when you use it to infuse an oil with its delicate flavor and then brush the oil onto grilled fish.

Makes 1 cup

large pinch saffron strands
1 cup light olive oil or pure
*   sunflower oil*

Put the saffron strands in a clean dry bottle. Fill the bottle with oil and seal with a cork. Leave to infuse for two weeks, gently shaking the bottle daily, before using.

TERIYAKI MARINADE

This Japanese marinade is wonderful for barbecued and grilled meats. Marinate the meat for at least an hour before cooking.

Makes 1½ cups

⅔ cup olive oil

⅔ cup soy sauce

2 tbsp grated fresh ginger

2 garlic cloves, crushed

1 tbsp grated orange rind

4 tbsp dry sherry

Above: *Flavored oils are a good way of carrying the taste of the summer through to your winter cooking, as the freshness of the herbs and spices is captured in the oil.*

Place all of the ingredients into a wide-mouth bottle or jar. Seal the container securely and then shake it vigorously until all the ingredients are thoroughly mixed. Leave the marinade overnight before using. It is best to store it in a cool place, out of direct sunlight.

WARNING: There is some evidence that oils containing fresh herbs and spices can grow harmful molds, especially once the bottle has been opened and the contents are not fully covered by the oil. To protect against this, it is recommended that the herbs and spices be removed once their flavor has passed into the oil.

Flavored vinegars

Fruit-flavored vinegars give a delicious depth to salad dressings, and if used sparingly, such vinegars will enhance the flavor of fruit such as strawberries and nectarines that are not quite ripe. All flavored vinegars are best used within three months.

RASPBERRY VINEGAR

Makes 3 cups strained vinegar
2½ cups red wine vinegar
1 tbsp pickling spice
1 lb raspberries, fresh or frozen
2 sprigs fresh lemon thyme

Above: *Raspberry vinegar.*

1 *Pour the vinegar into a saucepan, add the spice and heat gently for five minutes.*

2 *Pour the hot vinegar mixture over the raspberries in a bowl and then add the lemon thyme. Cover and leave the mixture to infuse for two days in a cool, dark place, stirring occasionally.*

3 *Remove the thyme and raspberries and strain the liquid. Pour the flavored vinegar into a clean, dry bottle and seal with a cork.*

LEMON AND LIME VINEGAR

Citrus-flavored vinegars are wonderful for tart sauces such as hollandaise.

Makes 2½ cups
2½ cups white wine vinegar
rind of 1 lime (preferably unwaxed)
rind of 1 lemon (preferably unwaxed)

Bring the vinegar to the boil in a saucepan, then pour it over the lime and lemon rind in a bowl. Cover and leave to infuse for three days. Strain and pour it into a clean, dry bottle, adding fresh rind for color.

ROSEMARY VINEGAR

Herb vinegars are excellent for adding flavor to dressings and sauces.

Makes 2½ cups
2½ cups white wine vinegar or
*   cider vinegar*
6 tbsp chopped fresh rosemary plus
*   some whole sprigs*

Bring the vinegar to a boil in a saucepan, then pour it over the rosemary in a bowl. Cover and leave to infuse for three days. Strain and pour it into a clean, dry bottle, adding a sprig of rosemary for decoration.

TARRAGON VINEGAR

Make it in exactly the same way as rosemary vinegar, but with tarragon.

Right: *Delicious flavored vinegars are quick and easy to make.*

Pickles and chutneys

No country store would be complete without a good supply of pickles and chutneys. They are easy to make and the perfect way to deal with a glut of fruit or vegetables. They add a delicious tang to bread and cheese or cold meats, and are always welcome as presents.

KASHMIR CHUTNEY

In the true tradition of the country store, this is a typical family recipe passed down through the generations. It is wonderful with grilled sausages.

Makes about 6 pints
2¼ lb green apples
2 garlic cloves
4 cups malt vinegar
2 cups dates
½ cup preserved ginger
2 cups seedless raisins
2 cups light brown sugar
½ tsp cayenne pepper
2 tbsp salt

Above: *Kashmir chutney.*

1 *Quarter the apples, remove the cores and chop coarsely.*

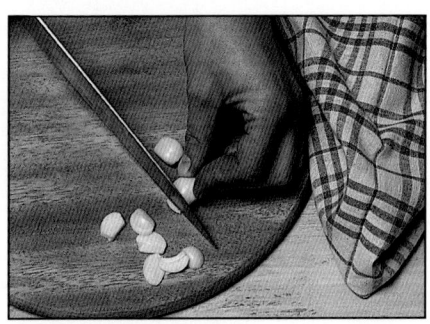

2 *Peel and chop the garlic.*

3 *Place the apple and garlic in a saucepan with enough vinegar to cover and boil until soft. Chop the dates and ginger and add them to the cooked apple and garlic together with all the other ingredients. Boil gently for 45 minutes. Spoon the mixture into sterilized jars and seal immediately.*

GREEN TOMATO CHUTNEY

Unripened tomatoes are a culinary success rather than a horticultural failure when transformed into a delicious chutney.

Makes about 5¾ pints
2¼ lb green tomatoes
1 lb apples
2 medium onions
4 cups malt vinegar
2 cups minus 2 tbsp. light brown sugar
1 cup golden raisins
1½ tsp mustard powder
1 tsp ground cinnamon
¼ tsp ground cloves
¼ tsp cayenne pepper

Quarter the tomatoes and place them in a large pot. Quarter, core and chop the unpeeled apples and add them to the tomatoes. Chop the onions and add them to the tomatoes with all the other ingredients and heat gently, stirring until all the sugar has dissolved. Bring to a boil and simmer uncovered, stirring occasionally, for one and a half hours until the chutney has thickened. Pour the chutney into warm, sterilized jars. Seal immediately.

WINDFALL PEAR CHUTNEY

The seemingly unusable bullet-hard pears that litter the ground beneath old pear trees after high winds respond wonderfully to cooking and can be used to make this tasty chutney.

Makes about 5 pints

1½ lb pears, peeled, chopped and cored

1 cup chopped onion

¾ cup raisins

½ cup chopped apple

¼ cup chopped stem ginger

½ cup chopped walnuts

1 garlic clove, chopped

juice and rind of 1 lemon

2½ cups cider vinegar

¾ cup light brown sugar

2 cloves

1 tsp salt

Place the pears, onions, raisins, apples, ginger, walnuts, garlic and lemon juice and rind in a bowl. Put the vinegar, sugar, cloves and salt into a saucepan. Gently

Above: *The merchants who brought spices from India also imported chutney recipes.*

heat, stirring, until the sugar has dissolved, then bring to a boil. Boil briefly and pour over the fruit; cover and let sit overnight. In a preserving pan, boil gently for one and a half hours until soft and thickened. Spoon into warmed, sterilized jars and seal.

DILL PICKLES

A must for the country store, these tangy pickles are made from prolific outdoor ridge cucumbers.

Makes three 4-cup jars

1½ lb small cucumbers
large bunch fresh dill
5 garlic cloves, peeled and sliced
3¾ cups white wine
  vinegar
3 tbsp coarse salt
6 black peppercorns
6 white peppercorns
2 bay leaves
1 star anise

Trim the ends off the cucumbers and cut them into 2-in pieces. Place the cucumber

Above: *The full flavor of fruits and vegetables is captured in these colorful and piquant preserves.*

pieces in a bowl of cold water, cover and refrigerate for 24 hours.

Drain the cucumber and, using a wooden toothpick, pierce each piece in several places. Pack the cucumbers into sterilized jars with the dill and garlic.

Pour the vinegar into a saucepan with 1½ cups water, then add the salt, peppercorns, bay leaves and star anise, and bring the mixture to a boil. Boil for five minutes. Remove from the heat and pour the liquid over the cucumbers and securely seal the jars immediately. If you prefer a sweeter pickle, add 3 tbsp sugar to the vinegar mixture before boiling.

PICKLED PEARS

Pickled pears go well with country-cured ham and buttery mashed potatoes.

Makes 2¼ pints

2¼ lb hard pears
juice of 2 lemons
1½ lb raw sugar
4 cups cider vinegar
1 cup water
3 cinnamon sticks
3 star anise
1 tsp black peppercorns
1 tsp whole allspice

Peel the pears and toss them in the lemon juice to prevent discoloration.

Place the pears in a large saucepan with the remaining ingredients and bring to the boil. Reduce the heat to a simmer and cook until the pears are nearly tender, which should take approximately 45 minutes.

Spoon the pears into sterilized jars and cover with the syrup. Seal immediately.

JACK'S PICKLED SHALLOTS

These shallots have a delicious sweet-sour flavor, with none of the harshness that is sometimes associated with pickled onions. If the shallots are blanched in hot water, they are much easier to peel, and if this is done under water, your eyes will be much less irritated.

Makes about three 2¼-cup jars

1½ lb shallots, unpeeled
bay leaves (1 for each jar)
2½ cups malt vinegar
¾ cup light brown sugar
¼ cup sea salt
2 tsp pickling spice
1½ tsp balsamic vinegar

Place the shallots in a large bowl and cover with boiling water. Leave for ten minutes, then remove the shallots and peel them with a sharp paring knife. Pack the shallots into sterilized jars. Place one bay leaf in each jar.

In a saucepan, heat the malt vinegar with the sugar, sea salt and pickling spice. Stir until the sugar has completely dissolved, then bring to a boil. Remove from the heat and add the balsamic vinegar.

Pour the vinegar over the shallots and seal the jars immediately. The shallots will be ready in two weeks.

Right: Preparing shallots becomes less of a chore if they are first blanched in boiling water and then peeled under running water.

ARTICHOKES IN OLIVE OIL

Artichokes, one of the few vegetables which are still seasonal, always add a touch of luxury to antipasto. This is a way to enjoy their delicate taste in the winter.

Makes approx. three 2¼-cup jars

2½ cups white wine vinegar
2½ cups water
1 tsp salt
2¼ lb small artichokes
2 small fresh chilis
1 tsp black peppercorns
2½ cups virgin olive oil

Have ready a saucepan containing the vinegar, water and salt. Trim the outer leaves of the artichokes, cut off the tips of the remaining leaves and trim the bases. Place each one in the saucepan as it is completed or the artichokes will begin to discolor. Boil the artichokes for about 10 minutes, until tender. Drain, cool and pack them into sterilized jars with the chilis and peppercorns. Cover with the olive oil and seal. Use within six months.

VEGETABLES IN OLIVE OIL

When vegetables are at their luscious best in the garden or at the market, they can be blanched and packed into large jars along with olives and slices of lemon. Covered with olive oil, they are the next best thing to bottled sunshine.

Quantity depends on amount of vegetables used

assortment of vegetables, such as peppers, eggplants, carrots, zucchini, mushrooms, broccoli and garlic
green and black olives flavored with garlic and spices
1 lemon, sliced
bay leaves
virgin olive oil

Cut the vegetables into large decorative pieces. Blanch each kind separately for three to four minutes, drain well and cool.

Pack the vegetables into a sterilized jar with the olives, lemon slices and bay leaves, and cover them completely with olive oil. Seal the jar and use within three months.

Flavored butters

Butter blended with herbs or other flavorings is delicious simply spread on fresh, crusty bread or as a garnish for grilled fish, meat or vegetables.

ROASTED PEPPER BUTTER

Roasting red peppers transforms their flavor; when combined with butter, they make a richly sweet spread that is ideal for picnics and barbecues.

Makes ½ cup

1 small red pepper
1 tbsp lemon juice
salt and pepper
½ cup butter, at room temperature
olive oil

Above: *Roasted pepper butter.*

1 *Cut the pepper in half and grill, turning regularly, until the skin is blackened. Remove from the heat and wrap in foil for 10–15 minutes; this helps to loosen its skin.*

2 *Remove the pepper from the foil and peel, remove the stalk and seeds and slice thinly. Place the pepper in the bowl of a food processor or a mortar with the lemon juice and a pinch of salt and pound to a paste.*

3 *Add the butter and seasoning and mix thoroughly. For a smooth paste, blend in a little olive oil, a teaspoon at a time, until the ingredients hold together.*

HERB BUTTERS

Most herbs can be blended with butter and used to finish cooked dishes. Try mint butter on peas, dill butter on fish or parsley butter on potatoes. These butters are also delicious when spread on cheese biscuits, added to stews for a velvety finish or used as a base for sauces.

Makes ¾ cup

¾ cup butter, at room temperature
¼ cup chopped fresh herbs
salt and pepper

Blend the butter with the herbs and seasoning in a mortar or food processor. Transfer to ramekins and chill for immediate use. Alternatively, spoon the butter onto grease-proof paper, roll up into a log shape and freeze for a couple hours. Unroll the butter, cut into slices and place in a plastic bag in the freezer ready for use. Use within two months for the best flavor.

LIME BUTTER

When topped with lime butter, a dish of simple grilled fish is given a wonderfully exotic flavor.

Makes ½ cup

finely grated rind of 2 limes
* plus juice of 1 lime*
½ cup butter, at room temperature
salt and pepper

Blend all the ingredients using a food processor or a mortar and pestle and chill for at least two hours before using.

GARLIC BUTTER

The most popular of all flavored butters, garlic butter can be used to enliven almost any dish and is the essential ingredient for garlic bread.

Makes ½ cup

4 garlic cloves
1 tsp sea salt
1 tbsp chopped parsley
½ cup butter, at room temperature
1 tbsp lemon juice
salt and pepper

Finely chop the garlic and blend to a paste with the sea salt using a mortar and pestle. Blend the garlic paste with the parsley, then beat into the butter with the lemon juice and seasoning. Alternatively, mix all the ingredients in a food processor. Transfer the garlic butter to ramekins and chill, or freeze, as for the herb butters (opposite).

ANCHOVY BUTTER

Spread on fingers of whole-grain toast, this is a sublime afternoon snack.

Makes 5 oz

12 anchovy fillets, soaked in milk for 1 hour
½ cup butter, at room temperature
juice of 1 lemon
cayenne pepper
black pepper
olive oil

Above: *Crusty French bread and flavored butters are all the ingredients you need for a delicious and colorful summer lunch, especially when accompanied by richly flavored olives and a fruity wine.*

Drain the anchovy fillets and, using a mortar and pestle, pound them until you have made a paste and then mix with the butter. Season with the lemon juice, cayenne pepper and black pepper, and to give the butter a smooth texture, slowly add a small quantity of olive oil.

Finally, pack the butter into a small jar or ramekins, if you prefer, and refrigerate. Be sure to use it within ten days. Anchovy butter also freezes very well.

Flavored salts and peppers

Flavored salts and peppers used to be very popular, but they are rarely blended at home these days, since we tend to rely on spice companies to do it for us. Flavored salts are easy to make and when fresh, have far more flavor than anything that you can buy at the supermarket.

CAYENNE SALT

This adaptation of an old Indian recipe produces flakes of dramatically colored and wonderfully flavored salt to use wherever you would use cayenne pepper. Remember, however, not to add any salt to the recipes you use it in. You could substitute chili or turmeric for the cayenne pepper, if desired.

Makes 3 oz
2 tbsp sea salt
¼ cup ground cayenne pepper
½ cup white wine

Crush the salt with the cayenne pepper using a mortar and pestle. Add the wine and 1 cup water to the powdered spices and pour into a bottle. Cork, shake well and let

Above: *Cayenne salt crystals.*

stand in a warm place for a week, shaking the mixture from time to time. Pour the contents of the bottle into a wide, shallow dish and place in a low oven or another warm dry place until all the liquid has evaporated. Scrape the crystals off the base of the dish and let stand overnight to allow any residual moisture to evaporate. Store in a sealed glass jar away from strong light.

LEMON PEPPER

Dried lemon rind mixed with freshly ground black pepper is a really interesting combination. Try it on grilled fish or in salad dressings.

Makes 4 oz
½ cup freshly ground coarse black pepper
grated rind of two lemons, dried

Mix the two ingredients and store in a sealed glass jar. This is best used within one month, before the flavors begin to fade.

Above: *Sea salt and quails' eggs.*

CELERY SALT

Celery salt is the perfect accompaniment to hard-cooked eggs, especially quails' eggs, which are delicious served as an appetizer with drinks. To make the salt, combine equal amounts of celery seed and sea salt. Leave both whole if you like a coarse texture. If you prefer finer salt, grind them to a powder using a mortar and pestle.

MIXED PEPPERCORNS

Black, green, white and pink peppercorns each have their own quite distinctive flavor. Mix them in equal proportions and grind them in the normal way just before use for an exotic flavoring. These will keep up to a year if left whole.

Right: *A nest of quails' eggs on a leaf plate, surrounded by flavored salts and peppers.*

Herb and spice mixes

Mixed herbs and spices are readily available in the shops, and we tend to accept that these particular combinations of flavors are the ones to use, but there is no reason why you should not experiment with blending herbs and spices to your own taste. A mortar and pestle are traditionally used to blend the herbs, but using an electric coffee grinder is an easy way to achieve very good results.

LEMON MIX

This combination of lemon flavors makes a wonderful dry marinade for chicken, to be rubbed onto the skin about one hour before roasting or barbecuing.

Makes about ¼ cup
2 lemons
2 tbsp lemon thyme, chopped
1 tbsp lemon verbena, chopped
1 tbsp lemongrass, chopped

Above: *Lemon mix.*

1 *Peel the lemons into strips and air-dry the rind and herbs on a rack for one or two days.*

2 *When thoroughly dry, powder the lemon rind using a mortar and pestle. Add the other flavorings, then crush and blend them together to the desired texture.*

3 *Pack the powdered herbs into muslin bags.*

QUATRE EPICES

This blend of four spices is traditionally used in France for flavoring sausages, pâtés and terrines.

7 parts freshly ground black pepper
1 part freshly grated nutmeg
1 part ground cinnamon
1 part ground cloves

Blend the spices together and pack them into a glass jar. Seal and store away from the light. Use within six months.

MIXED SWEET SPICES

The packaged mixed sweet spices that are available are extremely bland compared with a batch that has been freshly ground and blended. Make it in relatively small quantities and, as with the *quatre épices*, store it in sealed containers away from the light and use within six months. It is a good idea to label the spices with the date they were made so that you know when it is time to throw them out and make a fresh batch.

2 parts dried gingerroot
1 part white peppercorns or allspice berries
1 part cloves
1 part nutmeg
1 part cinnamon stick

Grind the whole spices and then blend them together.

Right: *Keep your herbs and spices whole and prepare them only when you need them.*

Flavored mustards

Making your own mustard is surprisingly easy, and just as with other freshly ground spices, the flavor is far more intense and aromatic than the ready-made versions.

TARRAGON AND CHAMPAGNE MUSTARD

This delicately flavored mustard is very good with cold seafood or chicken.

Makes about 1 cup

2 tbsp mustard seed
5 tbsp champagne vinegar
½ cup dry mustard powder
½ cup light brown sugar
½ tsp salt
3½ tbsp virgin olive oil
¼ cup chopped fresh tarragon

Soak the mustard seeds overnight in the vinegar. Pour the mixture into the bowl of a blender, add the mustard powder, sugar and salt and blend until smooth. Slowly add the oil while continuing to blend. Stir in the tarragon. Pour the mustard into sterilized jars, seal and store in a cool place.

HONEY MUSTARD

Honey mustard is richly flavored and is delicious in sauces and salad dressings.

Makes about 2 cups

1 cup mustard seeds
1 tbsp ground cinnamon
½ tsp ground ginger
1¼ cups white wine vinegar
6 tbsp dark honey

Combine the mustard seeds with the spices. Cover with the vinegar and let soak overnight. Place the mixture in a mortar and pound until you have made a paste, all the while gradually adding the honey. The finished mustard should resemble a stiff paste, so add extra vinegar if necessary. Store the mustard in sterilized jars in the refrigerator. Use within four weeks.

HORSERADISH MUSTARD

Horseradish mustard is a tangy relish that is an excellent accompaniment to cold meat, smoked fish or cheese.

Makes about 2 cups

2 tbsp mustard seeds
1 cup of boiling water
¼ cup dry mustard powder
¼ cup sugar
½ cup white wine vinegar or
*   cider vinegar*
4 tbsp olive oil
1 tsp lemon juice
2 tbsp horseradish sauce (see page 42)

Place the mustard seeds in a bowl and cover with boiling water. Let stand for one hour. Drain and place in the bowl of a blender with the remaining ingredients. Blend the mixture into a smooth paste and then spoon it into sterilized jars. Store in the refrigerator and use within three months.

Right: *From left: Honey mustard, Horseradish mustard, and Tarragon and champagne mustard.*

Jams, jellies and honeys

Homemade jams, jellies and honeys are the perfect way to deal with a glut of fruit and have an intensity of flavor rare in commercial varieties. Some preserving sugars have added pectin, which means that the jellies and jams need to be boiled for only a few minutes to reach setting point. This simplifies the process, gives consistent results and means that it is quite possible to make a pot or two of jam in less than half an hour.

An easy way to test for the setting point is to spoon a little of the mixture on to a chilled saucer. If setting point has been reached, a skin will quickly form on the jelly or jam, which will wrinkle when pushed with the finger. Most jams will benefit if left to stand for 15 minutes before being ladled into jars. This ensures that the pieces of fruit are evenly distributed rather than floating on the top. Some of the following recipes require the use of lemon rind, and preferably unwaxed lemon rind. Provided jams and jellies are properly sealed, they will keep for at least a year.

CRAB APPLE JELLY

Crab apple trees are so pretty with their abundant flowers and glowing red fruit, and though their role in the garden is mainly decorative, this jelly is a delicious way to make use of the fruit. Serve it with game or use it to glaze an apple tart.

Makes about 2¼ pints from each
 2½ cups liquid
2¼ lb crab apples
3 cloves
sugar

1 *Wash the apples and halve them, but do not peel or core.*

2 *Place the apples and cloves in a large saucepan; cover with water. Bring to a boil, lower the heat and simmer until soft.*

3 *Strain through muslin or a jelly bag. Warm the sugar in a bowl in a low oven (250°F) for 15 minutes. Measure the juice and add 1 lb sugar for each 2½ cups juice. Heat gently, stirring until the sugar dissolves, then boil rapidly until setting point is reached. Pour into warmed, sterilized jars and seal.*

ROSEHIP AND APPLE JELLY

This recipe uses windfall apples and rosehips gathered from the bushes. The jelly is extremely rich in vitamin C as well as full of flavor. It is excellent with biscuits or toasted English muffins.

Makes about 2¼ pints from each
 2½ cups liquid
2¼ lb apples, peeled, trimmed and
 quartered
1 lb firm, ripe rosehips
sugar

Place the quartered apples in a preserving pan with just enough water to cover them, plus 1¼ cups of extra water for the rosehips. Bring to a boil and cook the apples until they are a pulp. Meanwhile, chop the rosehips coarsely in a food processor. Add the rosehips to the cooked apples and let simmer for ten minutes. Remove the fruit from the heat and let stand for another ten minutes. Let the mixture strain overnight through a thick jelly bag.

Measure the strained juice and allow 14 oz sugar for each 2½ cups liquid. Warm the sugar in a low oven (250°F) for ten minutes. Bring the juice to a boil and stir in the warmed sugar. Stir the mixture until the sugar has completely dissolved, then let boil until the setting point is reached. Finally, pour the jelly into warmed, sterilized jars and seal securely.

Right: *A winter sun illuminates the colors of the fruit jellies in a glowing richness.*

RHUBARB AND MINT JELLY

This is an unusual alternative to the redcurrant or mint jellies that are traditionally served with lamb.

Makes about 2¼ pints from each 2½ cups liquid

2¼ lb young rhubarb
sugar
large bunch fresh mint
2 tbsp finely chopped fresh mint

Cut the rhubarb into pieces and place in a heavy pan. Add water to cover and cook over medium-low heat until soft. Strain through a jelly bag. Measure the juice and allow 1 lb sugar for each 2½ cups liquid. Warm the sugar in a low oven (250°F). Pour the juice into a heavy pan, add the whole mint and the warmed sugar then bring to a boil, stirring until the sugar has dissolved. Boil to setting point, remove the whole mint and stir in the chopped mint. Bottle in warm, sterilized jars and seal.

DAMSON JAM

There used to be many damson trees growing wild in the countryside. Today they are much scarcer, but if you are fortunate enough to have a supply of damsons, this deeply colored and richly flavored jam would grace any breakfast table.

Makes about 5 pints

2¼ lb damsons
6 cups water
4½ cups sugar

Place the damsons in a pan, add the water and bring to a boil. Reduce the heat and gently simmer until the damsons are soft. Meanwhile, warm the sugar in the oven. Stir in the warmed sugar and bring to a boil

Above: *Dried apricot jam.*

again, skimming off the stones as they rise to the surface (most can be removed this way). Boil to setting point, then let stand for ten minutes. Pour the jam into warm, sterilized jars and seal.

DRIED APRICOT JAM

This is a jam which can be made at any time of year, so when reserves start to look low in late winter, make up a batch of apricot jam and dream of sultry summer months to come.

Makes about 5 pints

1½ lb dried apricots
3¾ cups apple juice made
from concentrate
juice and rind of 2 unwaxed lemons
3 cups sugar
¼ cup blanched almonds,
coarsely chopped

Soak the apricots overnight in the apple juice. Pour the soaked apricots and juice into a pan and add the lemon juice and rind. Bring the mixture to a boil, lower the heat, then let simmer for 15-20 minutes,

until the apricots are soft. Meanwhile warm the sugar in a low oven (250°F). Add the warmed sugar to the apricots and bring to a boil once more, stirring until the sugar has completely dissolved. Boil until the setting point is reached. Stir in the almonds and let stand for 15 minutes before bottling in warm, sterilized jars and sealing.

ORANGE MARMALADE

Marmalades have been made since the fifteenth century, but the early ones were very different to those eaten today. Then they were fruit pastes or "leathers," but nowadays they are jams made using the peel of citrus fruit. The Seville orange was the only orange available at that time and it was used in all recipes where oranges were required. Today we have a myriad different oranges to use, but the best marmalade is still made with Seville oranges.

Makes about 5 quarts

2¼ lb Seville oranges
1 lemon, unwaxed
9 cups water
9 cups sugar

Wash and quarter the oranges and lemon. Remove the flesh, pips and pulp, and tie in a muslin cloth. Slice the peel finely or coarsely. Place the peel and the muslin bag in a preserving pan and add the water. Bring to a boil, then simmer for one and a half to two hours, until the peel is tender. Meanwhile, warm the sugar in a low oven (250°F). Stir the sugar into the fruit until it is dissolved, then boil rapidly to setting point. Let sit for 15 minutes. Pour the marmalade into warm, sterilized jars and seal.

Right: *Clockwise from top left: Orange marmalade, Rhubarb and mint jelly, Damson jam, and Dried apricot jam.*

RHUBARB AND GINGER JAM

The best rhubarb for pies and tarts is the young, slender pink spring stems. Later in the summer, when the leaves have reached elephant-ear proportions and the stalks are thick and green, is the time to make this preserve. Use it with cream as a cake filling or stir it into plain yogurt.

Makes about 5 pints

2¼ lb rhubarb

4½ cups sugar

1 oz dried gingerroot, bruised

½ cup crystallized ginger

2 oz candied orange peel, chopped

Cut the rhubarb into short pieces and layer with sugar in a glass bowl. Let sit overnight. Put the rhubarb and dissolved sugar into a large pan. Tie the bruised gingerroot into a piece of muslin and add it to the rhubarb. Cook gently for 30 minutes until the rhubarb has softened. Then boil rapidly until the setting point is reached. Remove the muslin. Stir in the crystallized ginger and candied peel and leave for 15 minutes. Pour the jam into warm, dry, sterilized jars and seal.

LEMON AND LIME CURD

This sumptuously rich fruit curd is not diet food. Rather, it is a treat to be brought out of the cupboard for a special event or as a particularly wonderful filling for a roulade.

Makes about 2 pints

3 large lemons, unwaxed

3 limes, unwaxed

¾ cup unsalted butter

2 cups granulated sugar

4 large eggs, well beaten

1 Wash the lemons and limes and finely grate the rinds.

2 Squeeze and then strain the juice of the lemons and limes.

3 Melt the butter in a double saucepan. Add the lemon rind, juice, sugar and well-beaten eggs. Cook the mixture over low heat for about 25 minutes, stirring continuously until it is smooth and thick. Pour the curd into warm, sterilized jars and cover at once. Use within two months.

Above: *Lemon and lime curd.*

FLAVORED HONEYS

The finest honeys are those that are made by bees collecting from a single flower source such as clover, lime blossom or wild thyme. These honeys have great character but are also quite expensive. Commercially produced honey can be made a lot more interesting with the simple addition of flavors. The method is easy and the results are delicious.

Vanilla Honey

Immerse one split pod of vanilla in a small jar of clear honey. Let stand for one week, stirring occasionally, before using.

Ginger Honey

Slice a single piece of preserved stem ginger into a jar of clear honey. Let stand for one week, stirring occasionally. It is especially good for a honey-and-lemon drink.

Above: *Curds may be used as a spread, but they are also excellent fillings for tarts and rolls. Flavored honeys make an unusual but delicious preserve.*

Whiskey Honey

Gently heat a jar of honey, stir in 3 tbsp whiskey and allow the honey to set again. Try it on oatmeal for a really hearty celebration breakfast.

Candied fruit

Homemade candied fruit bears little or no resemblance in flavor or appearance to the packages of mixed citrus peel available in stores. It is so delicious that it can be eaten on its own as candy.

CANDIED PEEL RIBBONS

Make this in the latter part of winter when the new season's citrus fruit is available. It will keep all year and can be used in apple pies or baked apples, to enliven a bought mincemeat for mince pies or even added to a beef stew to give a deep, rich flavor. Any syrup that is left over from the candying process can be used in fruit salads or drizzled over a freshly baked sponge cake. To preserve the individual flavor of each fruit – lemons, limes and oranges – they should all be candied separately. The same process may be used to candy orange slices and larger pieces of citrus peel.

Makes about 1½ lb

5 large oranges or 10 lemons or limes,
  unwaxed
3 cups sugar, plus extra
  for sprinkling

Above: *Candied citrus peel ribbons.*

1 *Halve the fruit, squeeze out the juice and discard the flesh, but not the pith.*

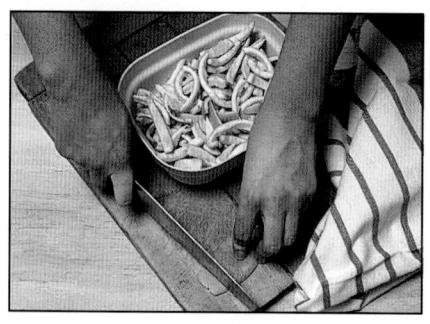

2 *Cut the peel into strips about ½ in wide. Place in a pan, cover with boiling water and simmer for five minutes. Drain, then repeat this step four times, using fresh water each time to remove the peel's bitterness.*

3 *In a heavy-bottomed saucepan, combine 1 cup water and the sugar; heat to dissolve the sugar. Add the peel and cook slowly, partially covered, until soft (30–40 minutes). Cool thoroughly; sprinkle with sugar.*

CANDIED GINGER

Now that good-quality fresh ginger is easily available, it is practical to candy your own. You can use candied ginger in cakes or puddings, or simply nibble on a piece as a treat.

Makes about 1½ lb

12 oz fresh gingerroot
1 cup granulated sugar
superfine sugar, for coating

Place the ginger in a saucepan. Cover with water, bring to a boil and simmer gently for about 15 minutes until tender. Drain the ginger thoroughly and peel when cool. Cut into ¼-in slices.

In a heavy-based saucepan, dissolve the sugar in ½ cup of water and cook, without stirring, over low heat until the mixture becomes syrupy, which should take approximately 15 minutes. Add the ginger slices and continue to cook over low heat, occasionally shaking the pan to prevent the ginger from sticking, until the ginger has absorbed the syrup. Remove the cooked slices, place them on a wire rack and set aside to cool.

When they are cool enough, coat the ginger slices with the superfine sugar and spread them out on greaseproof paper for about two to three days, until the sugar has crystallized. Store them in an airtight glass jar, where they will keep indefinitely.

Right: *Citrus fruit can be candied whole or in ribbons or slices, but however it is done, it is twice as good when homemade.*

PEACH WINE

This is not really a proper wine at all, but instead a delicious and refreshing amalgam of peaches, wine and eau de vie. Although you could drink it at any time of the year, it is really intended to be made and drunk during the summer, either on its own or diluted with soda water.

Makes about 5 cups

6 ripe peaches
4 cups dry white wine
Scant 1 cup superfine sugar
¾ cup eau de vie

1 Peel and halve the peaches, then poach them in the white wine for approximately 15 minutes, or until tender. Cover and let stand overnight.

2 Remove the peaches, then strain the liquid through a coffee filter. Add the sugar and eau de vie and stir to dissolve the sugar.

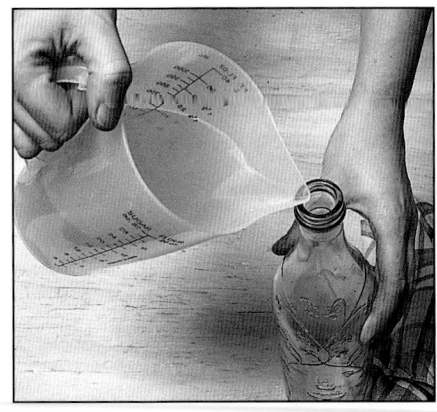

3 Pour the wine into clean, dry, sterilized bottles and cork. Store in the refrigerator. Drink within two weeks. Serve well chilled.

Above: *Peach wine.*

MULBERRY RATAFIA

Ten years ago, I was lucky enough to have a glut of mulberries and I transformed some of the fruit into this delicious drink. There are still a couple bottles left and the fresh mulberry taste has not diminished at all over the years.

Quantity depends on the amount of fruit picked

mulberries
superfine sugar
vodka, brandy or gin

Fill clean, dry sterilized jars with clean fruit. Pour in superfine sugar so that it comes a third of the way up the jar, then fill to the top with the spirit of your choice. Seal the jars and shake them to help the sugar dissolve. Store for at least a couple months, occasionally shaking the jars.

Strain the fruit (which you can use to make a delicious apple pie) and bottle the ratafia in clean, dry, sterilized bottles and seal securely. It should keep indefinitely if stored in airtight bottles.

SLOE GIN

This is a real country drink, which was traditionally used to celebrate high days and holidays. Sloes are gathered from the fields after the first frosts and the first bottle is ready in time for Christmas.

Quantity depends on the amount of fruit picked

sloes
superfine sugar
gin

Wash the sloes, removing any stalks, bits of twig or leaves. Prick each sloe with a toothpick or needle, then pack the fruit into a widemouth jar or bottle. Pour in the sugar so that it comes halfway up the jar, then fill to the top with gin and seal. Shake the jar from time to time to help the sugar dissolve. Before drinking, strain off the sloes and decant the gin into a pretty bottle that is clean and dry.

Right: *Delicious and colorful liqueurs.*

Teas and tisanes

Before tea was widely available, country dwellers made hot drinks from the herbs growing wild and in their gardens, and found them good for their health as well as pleasant tasting. With the arrival of teas from China, they followed the example of the Chinese and added flowers and other flavorings to enhance the taste and appearance of the teas.

ROSE PETAL TEA

Another delicious drink for summer, this one is very pretty when poured unstrained into tea glasses so that the petals and tea leaves are visible at the bottom of the glass.

Makes 4½ oz
½ oz scented red rose petals
4 oz Oolong tea

Mix the rose petals with the tea and store in an airtight container.

Above: *Rose petal tea.*

Above: *Marigold and verbena tisane.*

MARIGOLD AND VERBENA TISANE

This attractive and distinctive gold and green tisane is reputed to be excellent for purifying the blood and aiding digestion. Why not try drinking some after a heavy meal? The verbena gives the tea an intensely lemony flavor and the marigold adds a peppery note.

Makes 3 oz
2 oz dried marigold petals
1 oz dried lemon verbena leaves

Mix the petals and leaves together and then store in an airtight container. To serve, all you have to do is infuse one tablespoonful of the tea in a mug of hot water, then leave it to stand, covered, for approximately five minutes before drinking.

ORANGE AND LEMON TEA

Citrus fruit adds a fresh zestiness to tea, and this blend, with its addition of dried orange and lemon rind, is ideal for drinking without milk on a summer afternoon. For an even more pronounced flavor, a few drops of orange and lemon essential oils can be mixed into the tea.

Makes 4½ oz

1 lemon, unwaxed

1 orange

4 oz Ceylon tea

Peel the orange and the lemon, cut the rind into fine ribbons then allow it to dry slowly in a warm place. Mix the dried rind with the tea and store in an airtight container.

CHAMOMILE AND PEPPERMINT TISANE

This is a perfect bedtime drink, since chamomile is a gentle sedative and peppermint is an excellent aid to digestion.

Makes 3½ oz

3 oz chamomile flowers

1 oz dried peppermint leaves

Above: *Try these teas and tisanes instead of your usual brew. They can be easily blended from home-grown herbs and flowers.*

Mix, store and prepare this tisane in the same way as the marigold and verbena tisane above. For the best results, always prepare your tisanes with hot but not boiling water and cover them while they infuse.

Baked goods and breads

Tea-time is often more than a just a quick cup of tea and a chat for most country people; it is a real feast with platefuls of teabreads and delicious cakes to stave off the hunger brought on by lots of fresh air and exercise.

APPLE CAKE

This is a wholesome and delicious whole-grain cake is ideal for ravenously hungry children who have just come home from school.

Makes 12 generous slices

½ cup unsalted butter
½ cup light brown sugar
2 large eggs, beaten
10 tbsp whole-wheat flour
1 tsp baking powder
apple juice for mixing
2 large eating apples, cored
1 tbsp raw sugar
1 tsp ground cinnamon

Preheat the oven to 375°F. Cream the butter and sugar until soft and fluffy. Then gradually beat in the beaten eggs. Combine the flour and baking powder and add them alternately with the apple juice until you have made a batter of dropping consistency. Spread the batter in a greased jelly roll pan. Thinly slice the apples and arrange them in rows on the batter. Sprinkle liberally with the sugar and cinnamon. Place the cake in the oven and bake for 30 minutes. Allow to cool, then cut the cake into wedges.

ZUCCHINI TEABREAD

The great advantage, and disadvantage, of having your own zucchini plants is the way they seem to be able to grow a new crop overnight. Eventually, even the most enthusiastic of zucchini eaters will begin to groan every time another dish featuring the zucchini is placed in front of them. However, this teabread is a cunning and delicious way to disguise the zucchini and is certainly tasty enough to win the approval of even the most vegetable-phobic child. It also keeps well.

Makes two 1 lb cakes

2 eggs
1 cup granulated sugar
1 cup peanut or corn oil
1 lb zucchini, grated
1 plain flour
1½ cups tsp salt
¼ tsp baking powder
1 tsp baking soda
1 tsp ground cinnamon
chopped walnuts,
* for sprinkling*

Preheat the oven to 350°F. Beat the eggs until light and fluffy. Add the sugar, peanut oil and grated zucchini and mix well to make a batter. Sift the dry ingredients and mix them thoroughly into the batter. Add the chopped walnuts. Pour the mixture into two greased and floured 1 lb loaf pans and bake for one hour, or until the bread is well risen and brown. Serve sliced and buttered.

BOILED FRUIT CAKE

The name refers to the fact that the fruit is cooked with the butter, sugar and tea before the cake is baked.

Makes a 1 lb cake

1½ cups mixed dried fruit
½ cup unsalted butter
½ cup light brown sugar
⅔ cup strong black tea
1 egg, beaten
1 cup self-rising flour

Preheat the oven to 350°F. Place the dried fruit, butter, sugar and tea in a saucepan over medium-high heat. Bring to a boil and simmer for 20 minutes. Remove from the heat and allow to cool. Stir in the beaten egg and flour. Pour the mixture into a greased 1 lb loaf pan and bake for one and a half hours.

Above: *Zucchini teabread.*

Right: *Clockwise from top left: Zucchini teabread, Boiled fruit cake, Apple cake, Yorkshire parkin, and Bread pudding.*

BREAD PUDDING

This is a traditional recipe for using up stale bread to make a tasty, filling snack.

Serves 6-8

8 oz stale bread
1¼ cups milk
½ cup mixed dried fruit
¼ cup unsalted butter, melted
Scant half cup sugar
1 tbsp pumpkin pie spice
1 egg, beaten with 4 tbsp milk
pinch of grated nutmeg

Preheat the oven to 350°F. Break up the bread and place it in a mixing bowl. Pour on the milk and set aside to soak. When the bread is soft, add the dried fruit, melted butter, sugar and spice and beat well. Stir in the egg and milk mixture. Pour into a greased ovenproof dish and sprinkle with the nutmeg. Bake for approximately 45 minutes, the pudding is until set.

MALT BREAD

This deliciously gooey malt bread is a favorite afternoon snack, great for when kids get home from school. Malt extract is available at health food stores.

Makes two 1 lb loaves

2 cups whole wheat flour
½ tsp salt
2 tbsp good-quality pumpkin
* pie spice*
¼ cup light brown sugar
2 tbsp fresh yeast
1 tbsp malt extract
2 tbsp soy flour
1 tbsp sunflower oil
½ cup raisins
1 egg, lightly beaten
* with a little salt*

Glaze

1 tbsp malt extract
1 tbsp apple juice concentrate

Mix together the flour, salt, spices and sugar in a bowl. In another bowl, mix the yeast with the malt extract, soy flour and 1¼ cups warm water, and leave to ferment in a warm place for five minutes or until the surface is quite frothy. Add the ferment with the oil to the dry ingredients. Mix well with a wooden spoon and then knead for five to seven minutes. Lightly knead in the raisins and transfer to a clean bowl. Leave to rise for 30 minutes, covered with a damp cloth. Punch down the dough, knead lightly and divide between two greased 1 lb loaf pans. Leave to rise for 30 minutes. Preheat the oven to 400°F. Brush the top of the loaves with the beaten egg and bake for 30–35 minutes. While still hot, brush the loaves with a mixture of malt extract and apple juice.

WHOLE-GRAIN LOAF

Bread making is wonderfully therapeutic: the kneading and the delicious aroma of baking bread are very calming.

Makes two 1 lb loaves

1½ tsp dried yeast
½ tsp sugar
1 lb whole wheat flour
1 tsp malt extract or molasses
1 tsp salt
1 tbsp oil
sunflower seeds or rolled oats
* for sprinkling*

Activate the yeast by adding the sugar and ⅔ cup warm water. This will take about ten minutes. Place the flour in a warmed bowl and make a well in the center. Mix the malt or molasses and the salt with ⅔ cup warm water and pour into the well. Add the activated yeast mixture and mix well by hand. Turn onto a floured surface and knead for about three minutes, until the dough becomes elastic. Divide into two pieces, fold each piece in three and place in two greased 1 lb loaf tins. Cover the dough with a dish towel and let sit in a warm place until it is well risen.

Preheat the oven to 400°F. Sprinkle the loaves with sunflower seeds or rolled oats and place in the top of the oven. Bake for ten minutes, then reduce the heat to 350°F and bake for a further 30–40 minutes.

Left: *Whole-grain loaf.*

Take the loaves out of the oven, remove one from the pan and tap the base: if the bread is cooked, it will sound hollow.

BRAIDED HERB LOAF

Flavored breads are wonderful with soups and salads. They taste best of all when made with fresh herbs and eaten in the garden in the summer sunshine.

Makes a 1 lb braid

1 tsp dried yeast
2 cups bread flour
1 tsp salt
⅔ cup warm milk
2 tbsp olive oil or garlic-flavored oil
1 tbsp finely chopped fresh herbs
  of your choice
beaten egg for brushing

Sprinkle the yeast on ⅔ cup warm water and let stand to activate for about ten minutes. Then mix the flour and salt in a warmed mixing bowl. Make a well in the center and add the yeast mixture with the milk, oil and herbs. Mix by hand to a soft dough. Turn the dough onto a well-floured surface and knead for about ten minutes, until the dough becomes elastic. Return the dough to the bowl, cover and leave it to rise for about one hour, until it has doubled in bulk.

Knock the dough back and knead lightly. Divide the dough into three pieces, roll them into ropes and braid together. Carefully lift the braid onto a greased baking sheet, brush with the beaten egg and sprinkle with some extra herbs. Cover and leave to rise for 30 minutes. Preheat the oven to 425°F. Bake the loaf for 35–40 minutes.

Right: *A braided herb loaf, miniature whole-grain loaves, and Malt bread.*

Sweetmeats and candies

Most modern children have no idea that sweets can actually be made at home. You will be viewed as something of a magician, and become just as popular, if you produce some of these delicious confections in your kitchen.

FRESH COCONUT CANDY

A coconut used to be a rare and precious treat in the country. Often the only way to get hold of one was to win it at the fair. The trophy was borne home by the victor to be transformed into delectable coconut ice, which would be divided into little squares and taken to school to share with friends. The squares can be wrapped individually in cellophane.

Makes sixteen 2 in squares

1 coconut
2 cups sugar
fresh coconut milk, from the coconut,
  approximately ½ cup
2 tbsp unsalted butter
red food coloring

Above: *Coconut candy.*

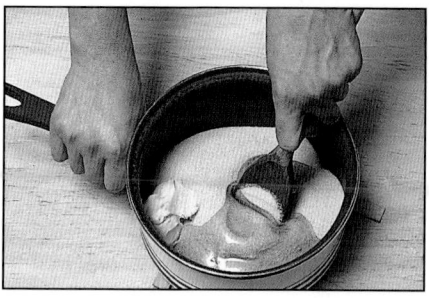

1 *Break open the coconut, reserving the milk, and grate the coconut flesh. Place the sugar, coconut milk and butter in a saucepan and gently bring to a boil.*

2 *Slowly stir in the grated coconut and continue boiling for ten minutes, stirring constantly.*

3 *Divide the mixture between two bowls and color one bowl pink. Then press the uncolored coconut mixture into a layer in a greased 8-in square pan, and cover it with a layer of pink coconut. Leave to set and then cut into squares.*

CHOCOLATE AND WALNUT FUDGE

Children love to get involved in fudge making. And with any luck, by the time they have licked the bowl and the spoon, they will have the patience to wait for it to be properly cool before devouring it all.

Makes sixteen 2in squares

1 lb sugar
6 tbsp light cream
2 tbsp unsalted butter, softened
6 oz unsweetened chocolate, grated
walnut halves

In a saucepan, mix the sugar and cream until you have made a thick paste. Add the butter and chocolate and stir well. Place the mixture over a low heat and stir it until all the ingredients have completely melted and thoroughly blended. Then raise the heat and boil for five minutes while stirring constantly.

Finally, remove from the heat and beat the mixture until it is thick. Pour it into a previously buttered 8-in square pan. Before the fudge has completely cooled, cut it into squares and place a walnut half on top of each square.

TRUFFLES

Making truffles at home is easier than you think and can be great fun for all the family. However, they are fairly rich and are definitely something of a treat to be brought out on special occasions. They freeze very successfully.

Makes 20 truffles
8 oz plain chocolate
6 tablespoons unsalted butter
1 egg yolk
cocoa powder for dusting

Above: *Homemade candies may be a wicked indulgence in these health-conscious days, but everyone deserves a treat now and then.*

Break up the chocolate and melt it with the butter in a double boiler, stirring to make sure that they are thoroughly blended. Remove from the heat and stir in the egg yolk. Place the mixture in the refrigerator until it is firm enough to shape. Then roll the mixture into balls and roll these in the cocoa powder. Place each truffle in a paper candy wrapper. Keep them in the refrigerator and use within one week.

The Bathroom

A selection of traditional creams, lotions and other natural
beauty products to scent your bath and pamper your skin.

Making cosmetics

Cosmetics is another area of our modern life that we have handed over to the "experts." While it is true that many of today's products are more pleasing in texture and smell than earlier creams and lotions, it is also true that they are nearly all made from the same, easily obtainable basic ingredients and that we are paying more for the seductive packaging than for the contents. It can also be very rewarding to use your own homemade creams and lotions. The simplest of the techniques in this section involves the mixing of like with like, for example, diluting an herbal infusion with rosewater, or blending a carrier oil with essential oils.

CHOOSING AND USING SAFE INGREDIENTS

I have tried to ensure that all the ingredients in this section are readily available. Inevitably, some are harder to find than others, but your local pharmacist may be prepared to order them for you. Dried herbs can be bought by mail order (see list of suppliers, pages 156 and 157). When buying essential oils, it is very important that you purchase from companies with established reputations, since oils can vary enormously in quality. Although the ingredients in this section have been chosen with safety in mind, it is advisable to do a patch test on you skin with the cream or lotion before using it.

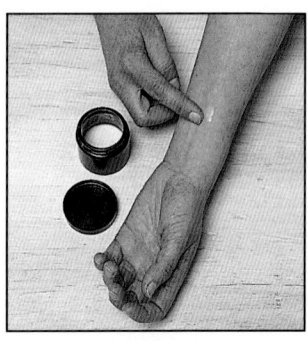

Left: *To test that your home-made cosmetics do not cause an allergic reaction, spread a small amount on your inner arm and leave on for 24 hours to see whether there is an adverse reaction, such as a rash.*

WARNING: Certain essential oils should not be handled by anyone who may be pregnant or who has an existing medical condition. If in any doubt, seek medical advice. Wear rubber gloves when handling the concentrated oil and spice blends to avoid any irritation.

TO MAKE A HERBAL INFUSION

Herbal infusions are very easy to make and are delicious to drink either hot or cold. Always store them in a cool place or in the refrigerator. You can also make infusions from flowers. Mix them with rosewater or witch hazel to make soothing or refreshing skin tonics (see page 92).

1 oz dried herbs or flowers or 2 oz fresh herb or flower

1 *Place the herbs or flowers in a pitcher. If you like, you can mix the herbs or flowers together, but always be sure the total quantity remains the same in relation to the amount of water you use.*

2 *Pour 2 cups boiling water over the herbs or flowers. Cover with a lid or sterilized gauze and allow to cool at room temperature.*

3 *Strain the liquid into a sterilized bottle and seal. A jar with a tight-fitting lid would do. Store in the refrigerator and consume or use within two to three days.*

MAKING CREAMS AND LOTIONS

Creams and lotions are slightly more complicated than an herbal infusion, since they require making an emulsion, which is basically a mixture of oil and water made with a whisk.

You will find it easier to make your own creams and lotions if you have scales, a measuring cup and spoons that can accurately measure small amounts. It is advisable to keep the equipment used for cosmetics separate from cooking utensils as the residues of oils and waxes may taint your cooking. A double boiler is essential for melting waxes because direct heat will burn them.

Once you have blended your oils and made your creams and lotions, store them in glass or china containers rather than plastic

Above: Waxes like white and yellow beeswax and carnauba are essential ingredients in many cosmetics.

Left: Keep your cosmetics in colored glass bottles to prevent light from affecting them.

ones, as the essential oils can migrate into plastic. Ideally the containers should be made of colored glass and always stored away from sunlight to keep the oils in good condition.

Herbs and flowers for health and beauty

It is advisable to use organically grown herbs and flowers whenever possible. Many herbs and flowers are safe to use and it is unusual to have an allergic reaction, but if you are in doubt, do a patch test (see page 76). Anyone who is taking homeopathic remedies should not use any of the mint family during treatment, because they interfere with the action of the remedies.

When selecting your own herbs for use, fresh or dried, pick them in the morning on a dry day before they reach the flowering stage. If you are drying the herbs for later use, they should be hung upside down, covered by brown paper bags or cones of newspaper. Once fully dry, they must be stripped from their stems and stored in dark glass jars away from any source of heat.

ORANGE FLOWER WATER AND ROSEWATER

Orange flower water and rosewater are used in many lotions and creams. In the Middle East they are considered to enhance health and beauty, and are drunk extremely diluted. They are a by-product of the perfume industry, obtained by distillation. The quality can vary enormously, but price is a general guide and the best rosewater is "triple distilled." Be cautious about very fancy bottles, which are sometimes used to disguise an inferior product.

Above: *To ensure that you gather lavender in its very best condition, you should pick it before noon on a dry and sunny day. In this way the herb will retain the full intensity of its aromatic qualities. This applies to all herbs. The lavender can then be tied into bundles and hung up to dry somewhere cool and airy.*

Left: *All fresh herbs, but especially those that have been grown organically, are wonderful, fragrant ingredients to use in all kinds of natural beauty products. They are also extremely rewarding when used to scent the bath.*

Right: *A very useful tip is to tie paper cones around your bundles of herbs, such as thyme, marjoram and oregano, in order to keep them free of dust and also to make sure that the plants retain their color while they are drying.*

Essential oils

The fruits, herbs and flowers described here have been used in the bathroom projects in this book. It is always important to double the dilution of any oil for use on children and babies.

HERB OILS

Lavender: Wonderfully therapeutic, this oil can be used undiluted on the skin to treat cuts and burns. Used in oils and lotions, it relieves headaches and aids rest and relaxation.

Ti-Tree: Derived from an Australian shrub that has long been used by the Aborigine people as a valuable healing herb, ti-tree oil (as herbalists know it) or tea-tree oil (as the public knows it) is an antiseptic, which is good for skin complaints.

Peppermint: This powerfully aromatic oil should be used sparingly or it may overwhelm. Peppermint tea is the best herbal treatment for digestive problems.

Patchouli: The oil of this plant, has an uplifting effect and is excellent for mature and problem skins.

Rosemary: Stimulating and invigorating, rosemary oil is one of the best treatments for any scalp problems. However, do not use it during pregnancy.

Chamomile: A gentle healing oil, which soothes and relaxes, chamomile is a good treatment for most skin conditions and is used to promote hair and scalp health.

FRUIT OILS

Lemon: Lemon oil has both valuable antibacterial and astringent qualities, and may be incorporated into remedies in the treatment of oily skin. It can irritate, however, and so should be used only in 1% dilution. Nor should it be applied to the skin before going out into direct sunlight, because it can cause discoloration.

Orange: Like the fruit itself, this warm golden oil imparts a wonderful sense of well-being and relaxation. Incorporated into skin-care preparations, it refreshes and tones all skin types. Like lemon oil, however, it should not be used before going out into sunshine.

FLOWER OILS

The finest of the flower oils are listed below: rose, jasmine and neroli. As they are all quite costly, it may be impractical to buy them all; instead, why not choose your favorite and use it sparingly – a very little goes a long way.

Rose: Good-quality rose oil can be bought in small quantities and is worth the investment for its incomparable fragrance and the fact that its gentle, soothing qualities make it particularly suitable for use in creams and lotions. Scented rose petals can be floated in a bath, or used to add color and scent to bath salts and skin tonics.

Jasmine: A sensual and fragrant oil that lifts the spirits, jasmine oil is beneficial to older skins. Like rose petals, jasmine flowers can be used to scent a bath.

Neroli: Made from orange blossoms, this essential oil is delicately fragrant and is also extensively used in perfumery. It induces a wonderful sense of well-being and relaxation.

Marigold: Although not used as an essential oil, this pretty garden flower's properties are used in creams for healing cuts and grazes (see page 110).

WOOD OILS

As the name suggests, these oils are derived from aromatic woods and have a resinous quality to them that is very attractive. Their fragrance is not overtly feminine and so they are suitable for use in oils and lotions for men.

Sandalwood: Sandalwood oil is used in skin-care products because it helps balance the production of the natural oils in the skin. It is useful in the treatment of acne and other skin conditions.

Cedarwood: Antiseptic and gently astringent, this oil helps in the treatment of skin conditions. However, it must not be used during pregnancy.

Frankincense: Made from a resin from the bark of a shrubby tree, frankincense oil is excellent for use in creams and lotions for mature skins, and to treat any skin complaint.

Clockwise from top left: *Lavender, rosemary, chamomile, marigold, jasmine, rose, orange and lemon. Essential oils are traditionally extracted from herbs, fruit and flowers by one of three methods: distillation, extraction or expression. Although the scale and apparatus have altered over the centuries, the basic methods are the same.*

LAVENDER BODY LOTION

This creamy lotion is perfect for treating dry skin in winter and can also be used to soothe sunburnt skin, as lavender oil is a very effective treatment for burns.

Makes ½ cup
¼ tsp borax
1tsp white beeswax
1 tsp lanolin
2 tbsp petroleum jelly
5 tsp apricot kernel oil
4 tsp cold-pressed sunflower oil
20 drops lavender oil

1 *Dissolve the borax in 2 tbsp boiled water. Melt the beeswax, lanolin and petroleum jelly with the apricot kernel and cold-pressed sunflower oil in a double boiler. Remove from the heat once the wax has melted and stir well to blend.*

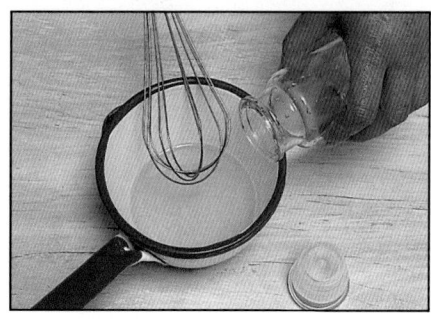

2 *Add the borax solution, whisking as you do so. The lotion will turn white and thicken but keep whisking until cool. Then stir in the lavender oil. Pour into a glass jar or bottle and store in a cool, dark place.*

84

PEPPERMINT BODY LOTION

This lotion is made as for the lavender body lotion, but using only 10 drops of peppermint oil. Use this refreshing and invigorating lotion after hard physical work. Do not use on small children or during pregnancy.

LAVENDER BUBBLE BATH

There is no need to buy commercially made bubble baths again. This bubble bath is quite delicious and so simple to make that you can prepare some extra as gifts for friends and family.

Makes 1 bottle
bunch lavender
1 large bottle clear organic shampoo
5 drops lavender oil

Place the bunch of lavender head down in a clean, screw-top widemouth jar. You only really need the flowers, so cut off any long stalks. Add the shampoo and the lavender oil. Close the jar and place it on a

Above: *Lavender is a popular herb to grow.*

sunny windowsill for two or three weeks, shaking occasionally. Strain the liquid and rebottle.

HERBAL BATH BAGS

Hang from the bath tap and run hot water through these herbal bags to release lovely relaxing scents.

Makes 3 bags
three 9-in diameter muslin circles
6 tbsp bran
1 tbsp lavender flowers
1 tbsp chamomile flowers
1 tbsp rosemary tips
3 small rubber bands
3 yd narrow ribbon or twine

Place two tablespoons of bran in the center of each circle of muslin. Add lavender to one, chamomile to a second and rosemary to a third. Gather the material up, close with a rubber band and tie with ribbon.

Right: *Lavender body lotion.*

Bath oils and scrubs

Lying in a bath of fragrant scented oils or exfoliating and nourishing the skin with a scrub are not traditional pastimes for country dwellers. In the past, bathrooms were extremely basic or even nonexistent, and bathing was for cleanliness rather than pleasure. But now that modern bathrooms are generally warm and comfortable, as well as functional, these activities can be enjoyed and make a pleasurable reward for a hard afternoon's work digging or harvesting in the garden. Of course, big fluffy towels that are warm from the dryer are also essential!

LUXURIOUS BODY SCRUB

This is a delightful alternative to the loofah, much more gentle and pleasantly aromatic. After a bath, dry yourself thoroughly and rub the mixture into your skin, paying particular attention to dry skin areas. Leave it to dry on the skin and then rub off using a soft washcloth while standing in the bath. It will leave your skin feeling soft and clean. It can be stored in the bathroom in pretty shell containers.

Makes about 5 oz

2 tbsp powdered orange rind

3 tbsp ground almonds

2 tbsp oatmeal

1 tbsp red rose petals

about 6 tbsp almond oil

5 drops flower oil (jasmine, rose, neroli or lavender)

5 drops wood oil (sandalwood, rosewood or cedar)

1 *Blend all the dry ingredients together.*

2 *Add the almond oil a tablespoon at a time, blending to a crumbly paste. Stir in the essential oils of your choice. Store in a glass jar and use within two weeks.*

Above: *Luxurious body scrub.*

ORANGE AND GRAPEFRUIT BATH OIL

At the end of the day, a scented bath is a therapeutic treat. Choose the oils depending on whether you wish to be relaxed or invigorated. An orange and grapefruit bath will gently refresh you. Add one teaspoon once the bath has been run to avoid the essential oils evaporating.

Makes about ¼ cup

3 tbsp sweet almond oil

5 drops grapefruit oil

5 drops orange oil

Combine the oils in a bottle and shake.

Right: *Orange and grapefruit bath oil and Luxurious body scrub.*

Nourishing creams

The countrywoman has always known the value of protecting her skin, and these creams provide excellent protection.

TRADITIONAL COLD CREAM

This is an all-purpose cream that can be used to cleanse and soothe the skin.

Makes 7 oz
52 oz white beeswax
½ cup almond oil
½ tsp borax
¼ cup rosewater

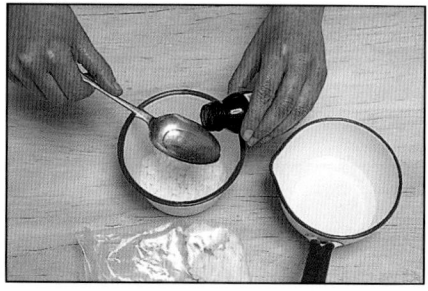

1 *Place the beeswax in a double boiler and add the almond oil. Melt the wax over low heat, stirring constantly to combine the ingredients.*

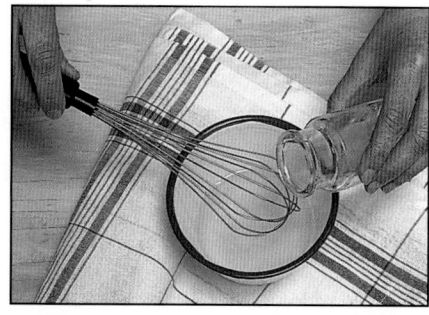

2 *Take off the heat and dissolve the borax in the rosewater and slowly pour it into the melted wax and oil, whisking constantly.*

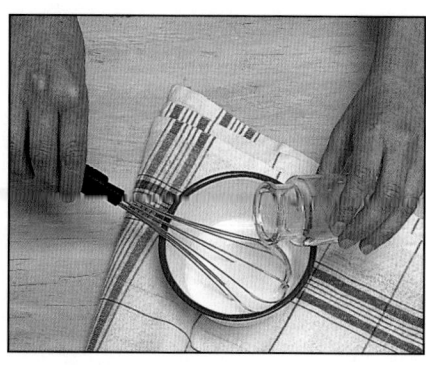

3 *It will quickly turn milky and thicken. Continue whisking while it cools. When it reaches thick pouring consistency, pour into glass jars or china pots.*

Above: *Traditional cold cream.*

ROSE-SCENTED MOISTURE CREAM

Rich in nourishing oils and waxes, this moisturizer is a highly effective night cream. If you have difficulty obtaining emulsifying wax, substitute white beeswax.

Makes about ¾ cup
½ cup rosewater
½ tsp glycerine
2 tbsp witch hazel
¼ tsp borax
2 tbsp emulsifying wax or
   white beeswax
1 tsp lanolin
2 tbsp almond oil
2 drops rose oil

Gently heat the rosewater, glycerine, witch hazel and borax in a saucepan until the borax has dissolved. In a double boiler, melt the wax, lanolin and almond oil over a gentle heat. Slowly add the rosewater mixture to the oil mixture, whisking as you do so. It will quickly turn milky and thicken. Take off the heat and continue to whisk as it cools and then add the rose oil. Pour the cream into glass pots or jars.

UNSCENTED MOISTURE CREAM

Ideal for applying before going outdoors, this simple, fragrance-free cream can be used by both men and women.

Makes about ⅔ cup
2 tbsp carnauba wax
1 tbsp white beeswax
½ cup almond oil

Melt the waxes and oil in a double boiler over low heat and stir. Take off the heat, pour the cream into a pot, and leave to set.

Right: *Antique pots containing creams.*

Cleansers and skin tonics

Exfoliating washing grains, flower skin tonics and gentle cleansers can be made at home for a fraction of the cost of many commercial products, and if kept in pretty bottles and jars, will look just as attractive on the dressing table.

ALMOND OIL CLEANSER

This gentle cleanser will leave the skin feeling soft and supple.

Makes about 1⅔ cups
2 oz white beeswax
1¼ cups almond oil
½ cup rosewater
½ tsp borax
4 drops rose oil (optional)

Melt the beeswax in a double boiler over low heat and slowly add the almond oil. Slightly warm the rosewater and dissolve the borax in it. Pour the rosewater into the oil mixture, whisking constantly as it emulsifies. Take off the heat and keep whisking as it cools. Add the rose oil if required. Pour into china pots or glass jars.

ORANGE AND OATMEAL WASHING GRAINS

If you like to wash your face, rather than use cleansers, this is a marvelous once-a-week treatment to exfoliate the skin and leave it feeling soft and glowing. Use the peel of organic oranges, because they will not have been sprayed with chemicals or waxes. To use the grains,

Above: *Orange flower and cornflower tonics.*

place a teaspoonful in the palm of the hand, mix to a paste with water and rub gently into the skin; rinse off and dry.

2 tbsp fine oatmeal
1 tbsp ground orange peel

Mix the two ingredients and keep in a lidded bowl or jar in the bathroom.

SKIN TONICS

Different formulations of skin tonics are used to soothe or stimulate the skin. Fine dry skins need soothing with delicate herbal infusions or flower waters, while large-pored or oily skins can benefit from a stimulating tonic containing witch hazel.

Skin tonics are made by pouring the ingredients into a glass bottle and shaking to mix. To use, pour a little onto dampened cotton wool and smooth onto the skin.

Each recipe makes 6½ tbsp

Orange flower Skin Tonic
(normal skin)
5 tbsp orange flower water
1½ tbsp rosewater

Cornflower Skin Tonic
(normal skin)
5 tbsp cornflower infusion
  (see page 110)
1½ tbsp rosewater

Elderflower Skin Tonic
(dry skin)
3¼ tbsp elderflower infusion
  (see page 76)
3¼ tbsp rosewater

Lavender Skin Tonic
(oily skin)
5 tbsp lavender infusion
  (see page 76)
1½ tbsp witch hazel

Linden Skin Tonic
(for mature skin)
4¾ tbsp lime flower infusion
  (see page 76)
1¾ tsp rosewater

Right: *The natural way – simple cosmetics made with pure ingredients.*

Hand creams and ointments

These emollient creams and ointments are ideal for hands roughened and sore from gardening and other country tasks. They can also be applied as barrier creams to prevent soreness.

WINTER HAND CREAM

This is a very nourishing cream made with patchouli oil, which is a particularly good healer of cracked and chapped skin. Why not try the old country treatment for sore hands? Cover your hands with a generous layer of cream just before you turn in for the night and then pull on a pair of soft cotton gloves. Your hands will have absorbed the cream by morning and feel soft once again.

Makes about 2 cups

3 oz unscented hard white soap
4 oz beeswax
3 tbsp glycerine
⅔ cup almond oil
3 tbsp rosewater
25 drops patchouli oil

Above: *Winter hand cream.*

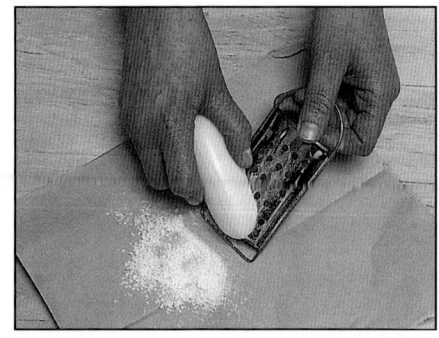

1 *Grate the soap and place it in a bowl. Add 6 tbsp boiling water and stir until the mixture is smooth.*

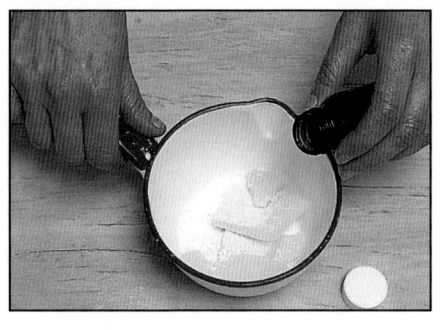

2 *Combine the beeswax, glycerine, almond oil and rosewater in a double boiler. Melt over low heat.*

3 *Remove from the heat and gradually whisk in the soap mixture. Keep whisking as the mixture cools and thickens. Stir in the patchouli oil and pour the cream into glass jars or china pots.*

Above: *Rose petals.*

HEALING OINTMENT

This is the perfect ointment to use on all the little cuts and scratches you get while working in the garden. It also works as a barrier against moisture and can be used to protect your hands when working outdoors in wet weather.

Makes 6½ tbsp

6 tbsp white petroleum jelly
½ tsp paraffin wax
¼ tsp anhydrous lanolin
10 drops essential oil (lemon, ti-tree or lavender)

Place the petroleum jelly, paraffin wax and lanolin in a double boiler and melt slowly over low heat, stirring constantly. Once melted, remove from the heat and continue stirring the mixture as it cools and thickens. Stir in the essential oil and store in a china or dark glass container.

Right: *Hardworking hands will benefit from regular skin care.*

Hair rinses and treatments

Both fresh herbs and essential oils can be used to promote hair and scalp health. Many of the hair products used today leave a residue which can dull the hair and affect the condition of the scalp. Regular use of an herbal hair rinse and an occasional oil treatment will restore shine and stimulate the scalp.

CIDER VINEGAR HAIR RINSE

This is a traditional country beauty treatment to invigorate the scalp and give the hair a deep shine. Use as a final rinse for the hair, towel dry, gently comb through and leave to dry naturally.

Makes 5 cups
1 cup cider vinegar

Mix the cider vinegar with 4 cups warm water and use after washing as the final hair rinse.

CHAMOMILE HAIR RINSE

This can be used by people with fair hair and also children. Use in the same way as the rosemary hair rinse (below). If left in the hair, it is supposed to lighten the color, especially when dried in the sun.

Makes 4 cups
2 oz chamomile flowers
⅔ cup cider vinegar
5 drops chamomile oil

Make this rinse in the same way as the rosemary hair rinse.

Above: *Store your hair rinses and oils in pretty bottles alongside decorative sea shells.*

ROSEMARY HAIR RINSE

Rosemary is a marvelous and effective hair conditioner, especially for dark hair. With the addition of some rosemary essential oil, this rinse is a natural treatment for dandruff and other related scalp conditions. You should use it once a week to promote and improve the health of your hair.

Makes 5 cups

2 oz rosemary sprigs

1¼ cups cider vinegar

10 drops rosemary oil

Pour 3¾ cups boiling water over the rosemary sprigs, cover and leave to infuse overnight. Strain the liquid, add the vinegar and the essential oil, then pour into a bottle with a stopper.

OIL TREATMENT FOR HAIR

Hair that is regularly exposed to the elements can become dry and unruly. An oil treatment once a month will work wonders for your hair and scalp. Use the oil sparingly on dry hair. Coat the hair rather than saturate it, and gently massage it in. Cover with a hot towel for 20 minutes, then shampoo off.

Above: *Herbal hair treatments restore shine to your hair and improve scalp condition.*

Makes 4–6 treatments

6 tbsp coconut oil

3 drops rosemary oil

2 drops ti-tree oil

2 drops lavender oil

Blend and store in dark-colored bottles.

The Pantry

Tempting ideas for scenting and decorating your home,
natural remedies and other recipes from the pantry.

The uses of the pantry

In Tudor times, in the sixteenth century, the pantry could be described as the control center of the domestic economy. It was here that the countrywoman would store her precious herbs and spices, and make lotions, potions and distillations. In doing so, she could be described as the family doctor, pharmacist, herbalist, perfumer, candlemaker and pest controller all rolled into one, and the health and well-being of everyone in the household was her responsibility.

Her knowledge was of a very practical nature, based on skill, observation and recipes passed from generation to generation. Her day, her week, her year were full of myriad tasks which had to be completed to keep her home running efficiently, and it is not surprising that few had the time, energy or learning to write down their recipes and formulas. From the manuscripts that do survive, it is clear that these women were full of common sense and a real understanding of the materials they worked with, apparently in marked contrast to the herbalists and doctors of the time, who were much inclined to invoke magical powers and use disgusting and dangerous ingredients in their cures.

Nowadays, potpourris, flower waters and scented candles are pleasing decorative accessories, but in the Tudor household they were essential to ward off dreadful odors and keep pests and disease at bay. Indeed, the scents they used were far from subtle.

Herbs were gathered, dried, stored and used in large quantities to add savor to food and disguise the less than fresh taste of most meat as well as for numerous medicinal infusions, distillations and for strewing underfoot.

Spices were precious commodities, carefully guarded by the housewife, who would keep them under lock and key and closely supervise their use. Although expensive, they were used in huge amounts: we would find these quantities quite overpowering, but like herbs, they were a disguise for rancid flavors. Their curative powers were also well recognized and respected.

The modern pantry projects are, in many ways, highly romanticized versions of their medieval equivalents. We make these things for pleasure rather than for practical purposes, nevertheless they are fragrant, decorative and sometimes functional. By passing on these methods, we help to continue a tradition that has been an essential part of country life for centuries.

Left: *Fragrant and colorful dried flowers are stored in glass jars ready to be blended with herbs, spices and fixatives to make aromatic potpourris that can be used throughout the home.*

Above: *If you want to use roses in potpourris, gather them before their petals drop. Spread the petals on absorbent paper to dry, then pack them in airtight jars or boxes.*

Right: *Aromatic herbs and spices have always been highly prized. In the past, wars were fought for control of the spice routes and the spice merchants were often men of almost limitless wealth.*

Room fresheners and burners

Once you have a range of essential oils, you have everything you need to perfume your house. Fragrance influences mood, and by using a refreshing oil like lemon or grapefruit, you can stimulate a feeling of energy and concentration, while a sensual oil like jasmine will create a romantic mood.

SPRAYER

You can dilute an essential oil using the ratio of 10 drops oil to 7 tbsp water and use it in a sprayer. If possible, use a metal or ceramic sprayer as the oils will deteriorate if stored in plastic.

VAPORIZER

The traditional vaporizer consists of a pierced ceramic bowl that holds a nightlight or candle over which is placed a small saucer of essential oil diluted with water. As the water is warmed, the oil is diffused into the air. Use a vaporizer at Christmas to create instant atmosphere by warming a mixture of cinnamon and orange oils.

CERAMIC RING

This is porous to absorb oil and fits over a light bulb. As the ring is warmed, the fragrance is diffused. There have been reports of these exploding (though I have never had any problems), so check on their safety.

DRIED ORANGES

Oranges, particularly Seville oranges, are fragrant when dried. Place some in a bowl to scent a room. When their fragrance begins to fade, you can rejuvenate them with bergamot or sweet orange oil.

Above: *Richly fragrant dried Seville oranges.*

Make a series of vertical cuts through the skin of each orange. Place the oranges on a wire rack in a baking tray and leave overnight in a very low oven with the door slightly ajar (the oranges give off a great deal of moisture, which needs to evaporate). Put the rack in a warm and dry place and leave to dry for at least a week, preferably more, until the oranges feel hard and very light.

POMANDERS

Pomanders have been popular since Tudor times because their fragrance is delicious and long-lasting. A well-made pomander will still give off its scent years later. Seville oranges are the finest for this purpose (select only unblemished ones; the cloves should also be the best). Hang pomanders in wardrobes and cupboards.

Makes 6 pomanders
4 oz ground cinnamon
2 oz ground cloves
½ oz ground allspice
½ oz freshly grated nutmeg
½ oz ground coriander
1 oz ground orris root
6 Seville oranges
4 oz whole cloves

Mix all the ground spices and orris root thoroughly in a lidded earthenware dish large enough to hold all the oranges. Stud the oranges with cloves, using a toothpick or large needle to make the holes. Roll the oranges in the spice mixture and leave them in the spices to cure. Cover the dish and stand in a warm place for at least four weeks. Turn the pomanders daily. If the spice mix feels damp, leave the lid at an angle to allow the moisture to evaporate. After four weeks the oranges will have shrunk and hardened and the pomanders will be ready to use.

DOOR SACHETS

This is an easy way to scent a room. Make small fabric bags (see page 106) and fill them with potpourri or cotton balls impregnated with essential oil (ensure that the oil is at the center of the cotton or it may stain the fabric). Fasten the sachets with ribbon or cord and hang them on door handles. As the door is opened and closed it will waft the fragrance around the room.

Right: *Fill your home with fragrances, which blend into a tapestry of natural, subtle scents.*

Scented sachets and bags

Like potpourri, sachets and bags can be used to scent your home. Use them in drawers and cabinets, tucked in among cushions and under your pillow.

LAVENDER BAGS

The most traditional of all scented bags, the lavender bag has enjoyed such enduring popularity because it is deliciously fragrant and keeps moths at bay.

Makes 5 bags

12 x 48 in fabric

needle and thread

dressmaker's pins

1½ yd ribbon or cord (optional)

filling:

3 oz lavender

1 oz ground orris root

25 drops lavender oil

1 *Cut the fabric into two pieces across the width, making one of the pieces 10 x 48 in, and the other 2 x 48 in. Cut each piece of fabric into five equal pieces. The larger pieces will make the bags and the smaller pieces will make the ties. Turn in a 2 in seam allowance on one edge of each bag and hem it.*

2 *Fold each bag in half, right sides together, and pin along the unhemmed edges. Stitch along the pin line. Turn each bag the right way out and press. To make the ties, fold the smaller pieces of fabric in half lengthways, pin and stitch along the side and one end. Turn the right way out. Fold in and stitch the unfinished end, then press.*

3 *Divide the filling equally between the bags and fasten each bag with a tie. Alternatively, you can fasten each bag with a 10-in piece of ribbon or cord.*

Left: *The ever-popular lavender bag.*

Right: *Use remnants and scraps for bags.*

ROSE AND LAVENDER-SCENTED CUSHION

Scented cushions are a charming way to perfume the home. They release their fragrance every time they are leaned against. The fragrance will last well, but make the cushion cover removable so that you can replace the mixture when the scent fades.

2 oz rose petals and buds
¼ oz lavender flowers
¼ oz oakmoss (optional)
5 bay leaves, crumbled
1 tbsp ground cinnamon
1 tbsp ground orris root
10 drops rose oil
16-in square piece of muslin
needle and thread
20-in square piece thick batting
20-in square cushion cover

1 *Mix all the dry ingredients in a bowl and add the rose oil.*

2 *Fold the muslin in half twice and make a seam along two sides to create a bag 8 in square. Fill with the aromatic mixture and stitch the opening closed.*

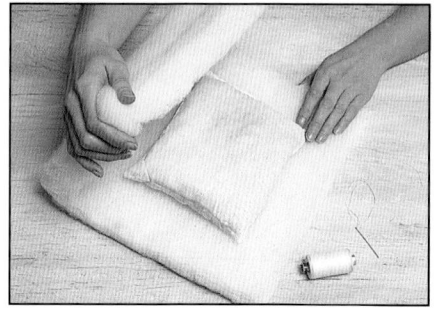

3 *Place the scented bag on the batting and fold the batting over the bag. Stitch around the batting to create the pad for the cushion. Slip the scented cushion pad into the cover.*

ROSE-SCENTED SACHETS

Make these wonderfully fragrant sachets in exactly the same way as the lavender bags on page 106, and then stuff them with the following:

3 oz scented red rose petals
1 oz ground orris root
25 drops rose oil

Above: *Scented sachets are a simple yet delightful gift to receive.*

MOTH-REPELLENT SACHETS

These miniature cushions are stuffed with herbs that repel moths. They can be tucked in among your clothes to protect them from attack. Use a mixture of equal quantities of southernwood (*Artemisia abrotanum*), tansy (*Tanacetum vulgare*) and santolina.

PEPPERMINT SACHETS

Sachets or bags filled with peppermints may help to alleviate nausea. An excellent use for these sachets is to carry them in the car as a comfort for children who suffer from travel sickness.

Right: *A scented cushion tucked in among the others on a sofa will release its delicate fragrance when someone leans against it.*

Natural remedies and medicines

In the past, the ability to effectively treat family coughs and colds, cuts and scratches was of vital importance to the country housewife, and she would pride herself on her knowledge and the array of lotions, ointments and infusions she kept in her medicine cabinet. The plants and herbs used then still grow wild in some of our fields, but few of us have the time and certainly not the knowledge to concoct the numerous cures and treatments, which made up her pharmacy. Nevertheless, there are some old-fashioned remedies which we can easily and safely use.

Honey and lemon is a tried and trusted remedy for most sore throats. To make it, mix the juice of a large lemon with 1 tbsp clear honey (or more, according to taste) and dilute with boiling water to make a wonderfully soothing hot drink.

Peppermint tea is a safe and palatable cure for indigestion and nausea.

Chamomile tea will calm restless children and ensure a good night's sleep for children and grown-ups alike.

Sage and honey tea is a comforting treatment for colds, coughs and sore throats. Add ½ oz sage leaves to 1 tbsp clear honey and the juice of a lemon, then dilute with 1¼ cups boiling water. Cover and leave to infuse for 20–30 minutes. Strain and serve the tea hot.

Calendula (marigold) cream is still popular as a treatment for cuts and scratches. To obtain an extract of marigold, tightly pack the flower heads into a widemouth jar, close and leave on a sunny windowsill for seven to ten days. Strain off the oily

sediment that forms at the bottom of the bottle. Substitute this extract for the essential oil in the healing ointment recipe (see page 94). Apply the cream to minor cuts and sores.

Witch hazel dabbed on to bites and stings will relieve the pain.

Cornflower infusion soothes tired and sore eyes. Infuse 2 tbsp cornflowers in ½ cup water. Cover and leave to cool. Strain, discarding the cornflowers, and soak cotton balls with the infusion. Leave on the eyelids for 15 minutes.

Garlic is a powerful, if somewhat smelly, antiseptic. Taken regularly in food, it purifies the blood and lowers cholesterol.

Rosehip and hibiscus tea is a rich source of vitamin C and will help keep coughs and colds at bay.

Elderflower and peppermint tea taken early will relieve feverishness.

Rosewater or orangeflower water added in very small amounts to hot water can be drunk daily to keep the skin clear and soothe the digestion. Only culinary-quality flower waters should be used in this way.

Left: *Healing herbs and flowers kept in the compartments of an old stone dish.*

Right: *Simple home remedies can be used to help treat minor complaints such as a cold.*

Scented polishes

Old-fashioned polishes are coming back into favor as we discover that spray polishes seldom give furniture the deep, glowing shine of a natural wax polish.

BEESWAX AND TURPENTINE POLISH

This is a very simple polish to make, and the addition of wood oils will give it an attractive resiny fragrance. Lemon or lavender essential oil may also be used in this polish. Apply the polish to your furniture using a soft cloth, let dry for a few minutes, then buff vigorously with a soft dust cloth for a deep, lustrous shine.

Makes 1 cup

3 oz natural beeswax
¾ cup pure turpentine
20 drops cedarwood oil
10 drops sandalwood oil

Above: *Beeswax and linseed oil.*

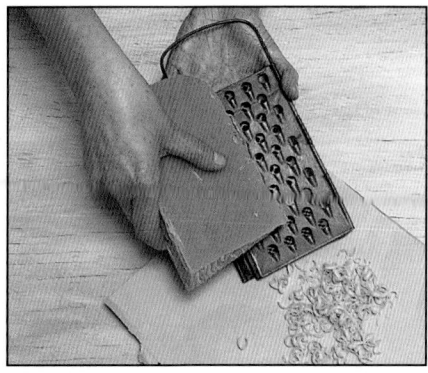

1 *Grate the beeswax coarsely and place in a screw-top jar.*

2 *Pour on the turpentine, screw on the lid and let sit for a week, stirring occasionally until the mixture becomes a smooth cream. Add the essential oils and mix them in well. The polish is then ready to use.*

FURNITURE REVIVER

Wooden surfaces can become grimy from a combination of dirt and a build-up of spray polish. Use this traditional country recipe to loosen the grime and feed the wood at the same time. It works best if it is used over a few weeks, since it will gradually remove the layers of polish, and once the surface is cleaned, you can return to a conventional furniture polish. Apply with a soft cloth, let sit for a few minutes, then wipe off with a second cloth.

Makes 3 cups

1 cup malt vinegar
1 cup pure turpentine
1 cup raw linseed oil
1 tbsp sugar

Place all the ingredients into a bottle with a cork or screw top, seal and shake well to mix. Label the bottle clearly.

CLEANING VINEGARS

Malt vinegar is an extremely versatile and effective household cleaner, especially in areas where lime deposits from hard water are a problem. At its simplest, vinegar can be used undiluted to give a brilliant clarity to windows and mirrors. Wipe over the window or mirror with a cloth or sponge dipped in vinegar and then polish dry with a crumpled-up piece of newspaper – this is an old but reliable way of achieving sparkling windows. Similarly, keep a spray

Above: *A selection of traditional cloths, brushes and polishes stands ready for spring cleaning treasured pieces of furniture.*

bottle of vinegar in the bathroom and use it to keep shower doors free of watermarks and to prevent the build up of lime on tiles, baths and sinks.

Rolled beeswax candles

Candles made from sheets of beeswax are very easy to make, beautiful to look at and aromatic to burn. Good-quality beeswax retains a strong scent of honey and the sweet smell will fill the room when the candles are lit. The wax should be at room temperature before rolling, otherwise it may be difficult to work with. A hair dryer set at a low temperature will help soften the wax without melting it.

Makes one candle

9-in length of wick
8 x 13¾-in sheet of beeswax
melted beeswax for brushing
paintbrush

Above: *A fragrant beeswax candle.*

1 *Lay the wick across the width of the beeswax sheet and cut it to length.*

2 *Gently fold the wax over the wick and roll the sheet into a cylinder.*

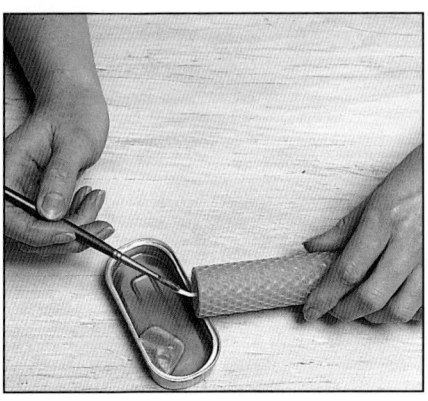

3 *Prime the protruding wick by brushing it with melted wax.*

SCENTED CANDLES

Candles that look beautiful and smell wonderful are my favorite way to scent a room. When making them, essential oils can be used singly or combined to create the fragrance of your choice. Old terra-cotta pots make simple but good-looking molds for the candles and can be used again and again. Scent with flower oils for a candlelit dinner, citronella or rosemary to keep insects at bay on a summer's evening and frankincense for festivals.

Fills one 4 in pot

small piece of putty or clay
4 oz paraffin wax
1 oz beeswax
6 in of ¾ in wick
25 drops essential oil

Block the hole in the base of the pot with the putty or clay. Melt the paraffin and beeswax together in a double boiler over low heat. Add the essential oil.

Dip the wick into the melted wax, then push the end of the wick into the clay or putty and position it centrally in the pot. Pour the melted wax into the pot. Drape the end of the wick over a spoon handle or stick laid on the rim of the pot to hold it in its central position while the wax sets. As the wax cools, a dip will form around the wick. Fill this with more wax if you wish.

Right: *The soft glow of candlelight is flattering and relaxing, and if you have a good stock of candles, you can easily create a mysterious and romantic ambience.*

Garlands and swags

As the seasons change, so do the flowers and natural decorations in the country home: the daffodils and bluebells of spring; the cow parsley and dog roses of summer; and the brightly colored berries of the fall. Other natural decorations also make their way indoors: fall leaves gathered while walking down the lane and brought indoors as precious treasures, an abandoned bird's nest found in a winter shrub or a basket of pinecones picked in the woods.

A MOSS AND TWIG GARLAND

Mosses and lichens are the predominant materials for this garland, with twigs, pinecones and golden mushrooms adding the finishing touches. I pick up fallen twigs and cones when I am out for walks but I buy all the other materials from good dried flower suppliers, and so should you, unless you have a plentiful supply available on your own land. When working with carpet moss it should be torn rather than cut to ensure that pieces join up in a natural-looking way.

florist's wire
12-in straw ring
selection of mosses, such as carpet moss, oak-
*   moss, spanish moss, reindeer moss and bun*
*   moss, all used here*
German pins or pins made from bent
*   florist's wire*
glue gun and glue sticks
small cones
golden mushrooms
twigs

1 *Attach a loop of wire to the back of the wreath. Cover the ring with carpet moss, pinning it as you go, until covered. Start to position the other mosses, also pinning them.*

2 *Alternatively, glue the other mosses in place using a glue gun. When all the mosses are in place, add the cones, mushrooms and twigs.*

3 *Fasten the cones together by twisting a piece of wire in between the layers of scales at the base of each cone. Apply some glue to the base of the cones before pinning them in place.*

4 *Glue the mushrooms in position and use pins to fasten small groups of twigs to the garland.*

A HERB GARLAND

A length of twiggy vine that has been twisted into a circle and tied in shape makes the base of this garland. Bunches of herbs are then tied to the ring with string to allow the herbs to be removed for use in cooking. Remember, though, that herbs exposed to direct sunlight and dust will not be as aromatic and tasty as those that have been stored in sealed jars in the store cupboard.

Above: *A herb garland.*
Right: *A garland of moss, twigs and cones.*

Above: *A spicy garland.*

A BAY LEAF RING

This is a lovely way to store your bay leaves. The ring below makes a simple decoration and the bay leaves are always at hand. The fresh leaves are threaded onto plastic-coated garden wire, which is twisted into a circle and decorated with a raffia bow.

Above: *A bay leaf ring.*

A SPICY GARLAND

To make this colorful and flavorful garland, galvanized wire is shaped into a circle (coat hanger wire is ideal) and the chilis and orange rind are threaded on. The chilis and orange rind can be broken off to use in cooking or the garland can be treated purely as a decorative object.

A HOP AND HYDRANGEA SWAG

In the fall the hop bines are harvested for use in the brewing industry. They dry most attractively and can also be used to make beautiful natural swags to decorate beams or the tops of cabinets and dressers. During

the year their color will fade, so that by the following fall, you will be ready to take them down and replace them with the new season's hops. Hop bines are quite brittle, so it is advisable to spray them with water and leave them to moisten overnight before you work with them. They can simply be pinned in place or tied to sisal rope as they have been for this swag, which has been decorated with bunches of hydrangeas tied on with burlap bows. Poppy seedheads, pink rosebuds and pink peppercorns add a touch of color.

Right: *A hop bine decorated with hydrangeas, roses, berries and poppy seedheads.*

Basket of dried flowers

The summer garden is full of richly colored flowers, many of which can be dried. Even flowers such as buttercups, cornflowers and love-in-the-mist can be dried by hanging upside down in an airy place. A jug of these on a dresser will bring back memories of summer long after it has passed, while a basket of dried flowers is a constant reminder of the garden.

The secret of successful dried flower arranging is to build the outline of the arrangement out of florist's foam and then cut the flower stems short, so that you can pack the flowers in tightly next to one another and control the shape that you are creating.

It is also important not to fill the basket entirely with center-stage performers like peonies and roses, partly because this would make the arrangement expensive, but also because they create far more impact scattered among simpler flowers or greenery. Display dried flowers out of the sun and blow on them with a cold hair dryer every now and then to keep them free of dust. Dried flowers should be replaced at least once a year.

rustic basket, about 7 x 9in
2 blocks dry florist's foam
2 pieces florist's wire
glue gun and glue sticks (optional)
2 bunches pale yellow achillea
1 bunch pink achillea
2 bunches carthamnus
6 pale pink peonies
3 cerise peonies
12 cerise roses

1 *Cut one of the blocks of florist's foam so that it fills the basket and then build a second layer with the other block. Pin the foam together with long pins made from the florist's wire or glue them using a glue gun.*

2 *Starting at one side of the basket, begin to build the arrangement with groups of one type of flower or greenery interspersed with the occasional peony or group of roses. Step back regularly as you work to check that the arrangement is taking on a balanced shape. Bear in mind that the flowers may be viewed from a low angle and crouch down to check that there are no gaps that need filling around the edge of the basket.*

Above: *Mass the flowers for a full effect.*

A TERRA-COTTA POT OF FLOWERS

An old terra-cotta pot is a sympathetic container for a small group of dried flowers. An arrangement like this is perfect for a bedside table in a guest room or as a gift to remind a friend of your summer garden. As with the basket (above), the shape of the arrangement is built out of foam, which is cut into a dome shape above the edge of the

Above: *Dried flowers in a terra-cotta pot.*

Above: *An arrangement should feature groups of flowers to create blocks of color.*

pot. Very short-stemmed flowers are then pushed into position. To ensure the flowers stay in place, use a glue gun to apply a little glue to their base. For this arrangement, carpet moss has been tucked under the flowers and glued to the pot to complete the natural effect.

121

Natural decorations and treats

BIRD NUT BALL

In the late fall and winter months, the birds in the garden appreciate extra food to help them through the cold weather and we enjoy the sight of them regularly visiting the bird feeder. Use this as an opportunity to clear out your kitchen cabinets, so you can replace any stale nuts and dried fruits before you start preparing for Christmas baking in earnest.

*equal quantities melted fat and bread-
   crumbs*
nuts, seeds and dried fruit
string
dried apricots
peanuts in their shells

Combine the melted fat and breadcrumbs and stir in half the nuts, seeds and dried fruit. As the mixture starts to solidify, shape it into a ball around a length of string and place in the refrigerator to harden. Place the remainder of the fruit, seeds and nuts on a piece of newspaper and roll the hardened ball around on it until it is completely covered with the mixture. Make a loop

Above: *Autumn nuts.*

from the string that protrudes from one side of the ball and thread apricots and peanuts in their shells onto the string on the other side of the ball. Hang the bird treat from your bird feeder or a tree branch.

FRUITY TREE

Glycerined leaves make a perfect foundation for any dried topiary. You can buy them in branches, ready-glycerined for use, or glycerine your own garden prunings. Here they have been wired into bunches for a fabulous full look.

pruning shears
3 branches glycerined beech leaves
florist's stub wires
dried pear slices

Above: *A fruity tree.*

*florist's foam ball, about 5 in
   in diameter*
flowerpot, 7 in tall

Cut the leaves off the branches and trim the stalks short. Wire up small bunches of four or six beech leaves and twist the ends of the wires together. Pass a stub wire through the top of each pear slice and twist the ends together. Completely cover the portion of the ball that will show above the pot with beech leaves. Add the pear slices and put the ball into the pot.

Right: *Create a bird nut ball and give the birds in your garden a winter treat.*

Seasonal Celebrations

Ideas and inspirations for recipes and decorations to enhance
country festivals throughout the year.

Easter

Easter eggs and the Easter rabbit are both pre-Christian symbols of fertility, which have survived into the festival we celebrate today. In some country areas, the tradition of rolling dyed eggs down a hill still survives, and it is variously attributed to symbolizing the returning sun or rolling away the stone from Christ's tomb.

SIMNEL CAKE

Halfway through Lent, it was the custom to make a simnel cake, which would be brought out to celebrate Easter Day and the end of the lenten fast. I cannot say that I remember our family fasting during Lent, but we did enjoy my mother's simnel cake, which was part of our Easter celebrations, along with those other traditional Easter treats, hot cross buns.

Serves 8–12

8 oz all-purpose flour
pinch of salt
½ cup golden raisins
¼ cup chopped almonds
¼ cup chopped walnuts
7 tbsp candied peel
grated rind of half a lemon
6 tbsp crystallized ginger, chopped
¾ cup glacé cherries, quartered
Scant 1 cup unsalted butter
¾ cup superfine sugar
4 eggs
1tsp vanilla extract
2 tbsp brandy
apricot jam, sieved, for brushing
1lb 2oz marzipan
food dye (optional)

Above: *Simnel cake.*

Preheat the oven to 325°F. Sift the flour and salt together into a bowl. Add the golden raisins, nuts, candied peel, lemon rind, ginger and cherries and stir until everything is coated with the flour.

Cream the butter with the sugar until soft. Beat in the eggs one at a time, then add the vanilla extract. Gradually stir in the flour and fruit mixture, adding the brandy with the last of the flour. Pour into a lined 8 in round cake pan and bake for one hour, then reduce the heat to 300°F and bake for another hour.

Allow the cake to cool thoroughly. Store it in a pan for four to six days before decorating. To decorate the cake, brush with sieved apricot jam before rolling out the marzipan and cutting it to fit the cake. Decorate the edge of the cake with a marzipan plait and the center with marzipan eggs colored with a little food dye.

Right: *A feast for Easter day.*

HOT CROSS BUNS

These will be more fragrant if you use freshly ground mixed spices (see page 46).

Makes 20–24

1⅛ cup bread flour

1⅛ cup whole-wheat flour

1 tsp salt

2 tsp pumpkin pie spice

¼ cup unsalted butter

½ oz dried yeast

¼ cup light brown sugar

1¼ cups warm milk

2 eggs, beaten

½ cup currants

leftover pastry for the crosses

glaze:

2 tbsp milk

2 tbsp superfine sugar

Sift both flours, salt and spices together and rub in the butter. Activate the yeast with 1 tsp of the sugar and a little of the milk. Make a well in the flour and pour in the yeast mixture, the eggs and the rest of the milk. Mix by hand to a stiff dough. Add the currants. Cover and leave to rise for about two hours until doubled in volume. Punch down the dough, knead briefly, divide into 20–24 buns and place on a greased and floured baking sheet. Cover and leave to rise until doubled in bulk. Top each with a cross made from pastry (moisten the cross so it will stick to the dough). Bake in a pre-heated oven at 375°F for 15–20 minutes. To make the glaze, boil the milk and sugar to form a syrup and brush the cooked, hot buns with it.

DECORATED EASTER EGGS

This is an activity for all the family, and although children may prefer chocolate eggs, the excitement of dying the eggs different colors and revealing the patterns will have them involved and entertained. If you live in the country and have your own chickens, slip some of these eggs into their nests on Easter morning. Send children to collect them – they will be sure you have magical hens.

hard-cooked eggs

candle, crayon or piece of beeswax

dyes (food coloring, turmeric, spinach, onion skins and beets)

1 *Draw any kind of pattern you want on the hard-cooked eggs using a candle, crayon or piece of beeswax.*

2 *Boil the eggs for five minutes longer in the dye of your choice.*

3 *Pat the eggs dry with a paper towel.*

Left: *A basket of brightly colored eggs.*

Right: *Children will love decorating eggs.*

Halloween

The foods and decorations of Halloween are supposed to echo the occasion, with the decorations being scary and the food bringing comfort. Pumpkins are the main attraction, as they are transformed into glowing lanterns and their flesh is made into soups, pies and fritters. Let the children cut grinning faces in their pumpkins and line them up on the windowsills while you cut star patterns in your pumpkin using pastry cutters to make a table decoration.

PUMPKIN PIE

Many years ago a Danish friend gave me her recipe for a luxurious pumpkin pie.

Serves 8

1 lb pumpkin flesh
¾ cup light brown sugar
¾ cup milk
4 eggs
1 cup heavy cream
¼ cup brandy
2 tsp ground cinnamon
½ tsp ground ginger or grated nutmeg
½ tsp salt
10-in flan tin lined with short pastry, chilled

Above: *Pumpkin pie.*

1 *Chop up the pumpkin into small cubes.*

2 *Steam the cubed pumpkin until soft, about 10–15 minutes, and leave to drain, preferably overnight.*

3 *Preheat the oven to 350°F. Place the cooled pumpkin in a food processor with all the remaining ingredients and blend to a smooth texture. Pour into the prepared pastry case and bake for 1¼ hours.*

Above: *Colorful pumpkins and squashes.*

PUMPKIN FRITTERS

These moist and delicious fritters should be eaten while still hot, liberally sprinkled with cinnamon sugar.

Makes 16–20

½ cup golden raisins
brandy (optional)
1lb pumpkin, cooked and drained
¼ cup all-purpose flour, sifted twice
1 tbsp raw sugar
½ tsp baking powder
pinch of salt
rind of 1 lemon
oil for frying

Soak the golden raisins in warm water or brandy for about 15 minutes, then drain well. Place the pumpkin, flour, sugar, baking powder, salt and lemon rind in a food processor and blend until the mixture is smooth. Stir in the golden raisins, mixing lightly to incorporate air into the batter. Heat the oil in a frying pan and drop walnut-sized balls of the mixture into the oil. Cook briefly, turning once, until the fritters are lightly browned.

Above: *The Halloween feast – a laden table lit by glowing candles and lanterns.*

Harvest and Thanksgiving

In the New World, Thanksgiving has superseded the traditional Harvest Festival, which is still celebrated in Europe. Many of the trappings and symbols of the two festivals are very similar. Central to both celebrations is the giving of thanks for the safe gathering of the harvest.

A DECORATIVE WHEAT SHEAF

In pagan times, a miniature sheaf of wheat in the home would have been an offering to the gods; now it is simply an attractive country decoration. Traditionally, the farmer's family would make a corn dolly, a braided decoration, from the last sheaf of wheat to be gathered in and this would be brought indoors for the harvest supper and kept in the farmhouse until the next harvest. Many of the corn dollies were extremely elaborate and each family had

Above: *A flat-backed tin container of wheat.*

its own designs. This wheat sheaf is not difficult to make but does require a little patience to achieve a good result. It is made using bunches of wheat bought from a dried flower supplier.

4 bunches wheat
silver birch twigs
string

Undo one bunch of wheat and adjust the heads so that they are level with one another. Once you are satisfied with what you have done, firmly tie the bunch together halfway down the stems. Repeat with two more of the bunches then tie the three completed bunches into one large bunch. Use the remaining bunch of wheat as the outer layer of the wheat sheaf and tie it in place. Trim the base of the stems level so that the sheaf will stand upright. Twist the silver birch twigs into and around the wheat sheaf and tie them in place.

HEART OF WHEAT

Fashion a heart at harvest time, when wheat is plentiful, for a delightful decoration that would look good adorning a wall or a dresser at any time of the year. Despite its delicate feathery appearance, this heart is quite robust and should last many years.

scissors
heavy-gauge garden wire, or similar
florist's tape
florist's wire
large bundle of wheat ears

Above: *Heart of wheat.*

Cut three long lengths of heavy-gauge wire and bend them into a heart shape. Twist the ends together at the bottom. Bind the wire heart shape with florist's tape. Using florist's wire, make enough small bundles of wheat ears to cover the wire heart shape densely. Leave a short length of wire at each end for fixing to the heart shape. Starting at the bottom, tape the first bundle of wheat ears to the heart. Place the second bundle farther up the heart shape behind the first, and tape it in position. Alternate the angle of the bundle of wheat as you work. Continue until the whole heart is covered. For the bottom, wire together about six bunches of wheat ears, twist the wires together and wire them to the heart, finishing off with florist's tape to neaten.

Right: *An attractive sculptural wheat sheaf bound with silver birch twigs.*

THE HARVEST LOAF

The harvest loaf is traditionally displayed at the altar among the fruit and vegetables and other offerings from the people of the parish. In the past there used to be fierce rivalry between neighboring parishes as they tried to outdo one another with the intricacy and skill of their designs. Although there were many different designs of harvest loaf, the most enduringly popular was the wheat sheaf, symbolic as it is of the harvest and the vital importance of bread as the staff of life.

Above: *The harvest loaf is in two parts joined by the braided binding.*

Makes two 1¾ lb loaves

7 cups bread flour

6 tsp salt

1 tbsp dried yeast

7 tbsp warm water

sugar, to activate yeast

egg, beaten, to glaze

Sift the flour and salt together into a bowl and make a well. Mix the yeast with the warm water and a little sugar and leave to activate for 15 minutes. Add the yeast mixture and 3 cups water to the flour and mix thoroughly using your hands. Turn out onto a floured surface and knead until the dough becomes elastic. Place the dough in a lightly oiled bowl, cover and leave to rise for one to two hours, until it has doubled in bulk. Preheat the oven to 425°F. The high salt content in the dough makes it easier to work, but this bread is more decorative than palatable.

TO FORM THE LOAF

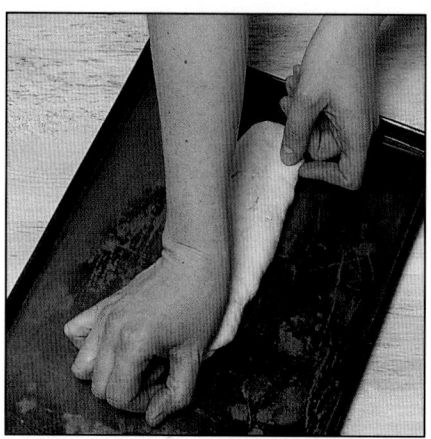

1 *Take approximately ½ lb of the dough and roll it into a 12-in-long cylinder. Place it on a large oiled and floured baking sheet and flatten slightly with your hand. This will form the long body of the bread, symbolizing the long stalks of the wheat sheaf.*

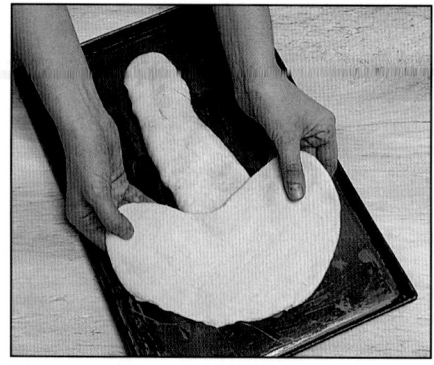

2 *Take about ¾ lb of the remaining dough, roll and shape it into a crescent and place this at the top of the cylinder and flatten. Divide the remaining dough in half. Take one half and divide it in two again. Use one half to make the stalks of the wheat by rolling into narrow ropes and placing on the "stalk" of the sheaf. Use the other half to make a braid to decorate the finished loaf where the stalks meet the ears of wheat.*

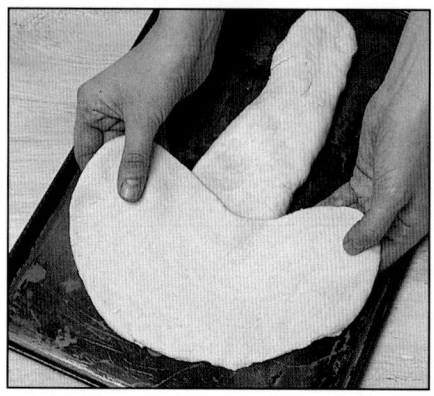

3 *Use the remaining dough to make the ears of wheat. Roll it into small sausage shapes and snip each a few times with scissors to give the effect of the separate ears. Place these on the crescent shape, fanning out from the base until the wheat sheaf is complete. Position the braid between the stalks and the ears of wheat. Brush the wheat sheaf with the beaten egg. Bake for 20 minutes, then reduce the heat to 325°F and bake for a further 20 minutes.*

Right: *The harvest loaf.*

HERBED CORNBREAD

Cornbread is a delicious, moist, cakelike bread that is served at Thanksgiving in recognition of the importance of the maize harvest to the American people. This herbed cornbread, made with herbs of your choice, is a delicious variation that deserves to be eaten more than once a year.

Makes 2 in squares

¾ cup all-purpose flour
½ cup yellow cornmeal
¼ cup sugar
1 tbsp baking powder
¾ tsp salt
1 cup milk
1 large egg
2 tbsp unsalted butter, melted and cooled
2 tbsp finely chopped fresh herbs

Preheat the oven to 425°F. Sift all the dry ingredients together into a bowl. In another bowl beat together the milk, egg, butter and herbs. Add the liquid ingredients to the dry ingredients and stir until just combined. Pour the batter into a buttered 8 in square tin. Bake the cornbread for 15 minutes until it is puffed and golden. Using a skewer or a toothpick, check that the center is cooked. Cut into squares and serve warm with butter.

Above: *Squares of herbed cornbread.*

CRANBERRY, RAISIN AND WALNUT TART

This is an ideal dessert for anyone who is not wild about cranberries but feels that they are an essential part of the celebration and should figure in at some stage.

Serves 6–8

1 cup fresh cranberries
1 cup golden raisins
½ cup chopped walnuts
½ cup raw sugar
¼ cup maple syrup
1 tbsp brandy
grated rind of 1 orange
10-in flan tin lined with short
  pastry, chilled
2 tsp cold unsalted butter, cubed

Preheat the oven to 425°F and preheat a baking sheet. Place the cranberries and golden raisins in a bowl and mix well. Add the remaining ingredients, except the butter, and toss so that the cranberries, nuts and golden raisins are coated. Pour the mixture into the prepared pastry case and dot the surface with the butter. Place on the preheated baking sheet and bake for about 15 minutes, then reduce the heat to 350°F and bake for 30 minutes.

CRANBERRY AND ORANGE SAUCE

Cranberries are also from the New World, and this sauce, which accompanies the Thanksgiving turkey, has also become an essential part of Christmas dinner.

Above: *Orange is one of the flavors in the cranberry, golden raisin and walnut tart.*

Makes 2 cups

1 cup cranberries
¾ cup fresh orange juice
½ cup sugar
2 tbsp Grand Marnier
1 tsp grated orange rind

Cook the cranberries in the orange juice until they are soft; this should take approximately five minutes. Then remove them from the heat and add the remaining ingredients. Finally, spoon the sauce into clean, dry jars and cover. Keep the sauce in the refrigerator until used.

It is vitally important to make sure that you do not overcook this sauce, which it is quite easy to do if you are not careful, because the cranberries will then develop a rather unpleasant bitter taste.

Right: *The larder's shelves are groaning with delicious Thanksgiving food.*

Christmas

Most of us are nostalgic for the traditional country Christmas, even if we have lived all our lives in the city; each year we optimistically think this year's festivities will be the perfect Christmas – and just occasionally it is. A laden table will appear with no dramas in the kitchen or harassed cooks, the tree will look magical, the relatives will all love one another and the children will be filled with rosy-cheeked wonder. One of the secrets of an enjoyable Christmas is not to try to do it all. Christmas should be a celebration for everyone, even the organizer, and a few things done well will give more pleasure than tired and resentful hosts.

Above: *Cones and seedheads for the garland.*

A CHRISTMAS GARLAND

A colorful, welcoming garland on the door sets the scene for Christmas. The natural materials, such as moss and pinecones, create a wonderful texture, and wired ribbon will be able to stand up to all but the most extreme weather conditions. The coarse sisal bows make an interesting contrast to the luxurious ribbon bows.

1 *Use a length of wire to attach a small loop to the straw ring to allow you to hang the garland. Cover the ring with carpet moss, pinning it in place with the German pins.*

2 *Cut the blue pine into short lengths and pin them onto the garland.*

florist's wire
12 in straw ring
carpet moss
German pins
blue pine
12 x 12 in cinnamon sticks
6 large pinecones
3¼ yd x 3 in-wide ribbon
9 poppy seedheads
sisal string

3 *Wire the cinnamon sticks into three bundles and, using the German pins, attach them to the garland. Attach wires to the base of the pinecones by twisting them around the scales of the cones and pin them to the garland close to the cinnamon sticks.*

 Cut the ribbon into three pieces and fold each into a double bow using wire to secure the bows. Pin the bows to the garland over the cinnamon sticks and cones. Tuck the poppy seedheads into the folds of the bows and pin them in place. Tie three bows using the sisal string, fray the ends and then pin them onto the garland.

Right: *Soft blues and greens give this Christmas garland a Scandinavian look.*

MULLED WINE

In days past, when people rode on horse-back or took open carriages to their neighbors' houses at Christmas, mulled wine was a necessary restorative to the circulation. Today, most of us can travel in warmer and more comfortable conditions, but the taste and aroma of this spiced drink is an established part of Christmas.

Serves 10

2 bottles smooth red wine
½ tsp whole allspice berries
1 cinnamon stick
6 cloves
½ cup sugar
6 drops Angostura bitters
rind of ½ orange

Place all the ingredients in a saucepan and heat gently without boiling until the sugar has dissolved.

EGGNOG

This spectacular Christmas drink is for some unknown reason far more popular in America than in Britain.

Serves 6

6 large eggs, separated, at room temperature
Scant 1 cup superfine sugar
1¼ cups brandy
¼ cup dark rum
2¼ cups milk
½ cup heavy cream
1 tbsp vanilla extract
salt
freshly grated nutmeg

Using an electric mixer, beat the egg yolks until pale. Gradually mix in the sugar until the mixture thickens. Whisk in the brandy, rum, milk, cream and vanilla. In a separate bowl whisk the egg whites with a pinch of

Above: *The heat of the mulled wine releases the fragrance of the cinnamon stick.*

salt until they make soft peaks. Fold the whites into the yolk mixture and decant into a serving bowl. Chill for three hours. Before serving, stir the eggnog gently and sprinkle with freshly grated nutmeg.

HOT BUTTERED RUM

A delicious alternative to mulled wine, this drink will warm the cockles of your heart.

Serves 6

4 cinnamon sticks
4 tsp light brown sugar
½ cup dark rum
2½ cups dry cider
2 tablespoons unsalted butter
rind of ½ lemon
½ tsp ground mace

Warm four tisane glasses or mugs. Place a cinnamon stick, a teaspoon of sugar and a quarter of the rum in each glass. Gently heat the cider without boiling and pour it into the glasses. Top with butter, a curl of lemon rind and a sprinkling of mace.

GLÖGG

Glögg is an extremely potent and dramatically pyrotechnical drink which is great fun to serve at Christmas parties. It should be prepared and drunk with caution as you will discover from the 144 instructions below.

Serves 6–8

4 whole allspice berries
muslin
4 cardamom pods
1 cinnamon stick
10 dried apricots, halved
2 bottles dry red wine
1 cup sugar cubes
2½ cups aquavit or vodka, warmed
1¼ cups cognac, warmed
nuts, unsalted
raisins

Tie the spices in a piece of muslin, place in a saucepan with the apricots and wine and heat. When the wine begins to simmer, remove the bag of spices and pour into a warmed heatproof bowl. Place a wire cake-rack over the bowl. Build a pyramid of the sugar cubes on the rack, making sure the construction is solid. Gently pour on the warmed aquavit or vodka and ignite at arm's length. Then pour on the cognac. Alternatively, ignite the aquavit or vodka in its pan and gently ladle it over the sugar. The sugar will melt as it burns and fall through the rack into the bowl. When the flames have died down, pour the drink into heatproof glasses or mugs, to which a few raisins and nuts have been added. Make sure that each person gets half an apricot.

Right: *The rich colors of Christmas are enhanced by the glasses of mulled wine, which have been filled to welcome guests.*

FRESH DATE CAKE

Make this wonderful fat-free cake each year as a delicious and light alternative to the usual rich Christmas cake. This is the perfect dessert to savor with a cup of lightly fragrant tea at the point when you never want to see another mincemeat pie ever again.

Makes a 2¼ lb cake

⅔ cup fresh dates
½ cup glacé cherries
½ cup self-rising flour
½ cup superfine sugar
½ tsp salt
1 cup coarsely chopped Brazil nuts
2 tbsp shredded coconut, fresh if possible
1 large egg
2 tbsp brandy

Above: *Stuffed dates.*

144

Preheat the oven to 300°F. Remove the skins from the dates, cut in half and remove the stones. Wash the cherries to remove the syrup completely and then quarter them.

Sift the flour, sugar and salt together into a large mixing bowl. Add the dates and cherries, nuts and coconut and then toss so that every single ingredient is well coated with flour. Whisk the egg with the brandy, add it to the bowl and mix all together thoroughly.

Pour the mixture into a greased and lined 2¼ lb loaf pan and bake for one and a quarter hours.

KUMQUATS IN BRANDY SYRUP

These lovely yellow fruits are highly decorative as well as tasting very good indeed. Make a few extra jars to give to friends and family, and why not spoil yourself and open a jar for a treat and eat a few of the fruits spooned over vanilla ice cream.

Makes 1lb 2oz, plus syrup

1lb kumquats
¾ cup sugar
⅔ cup brandy
1 tbsp orange flower water

Using a toothpick, prick each piece of fruit in several places. Dissolve the sugar in 1¼ cups water over low heat then bring to a boil. Add the fruit and simmer for approximately 25 minutes, or until it is tender. Drain the fruit and spoon into hot, sterilized jars. The syrup should be fairly thick; if not, boil for a few minutes, then allow to cool only very slightly. Add the brandy and the orange flower water to the syrup. Pour the syrup over the fruit and seal immediately. Store in a cool place and use within six months.

Above: *Kumquats and limequats in brandy syrup.*

STUFFED DATES

Slivers of crystallized ginger give a bite to these fresh dates stuffed with marzipan and topped with halved walnuts. They are delicious served with coffee. Packed into a decorative box, they make an unusual gift.

24 fresh dates
¼ cup crystallized ginger
4 oz marzipan
24 walnut halves

Using a sharp knife, slit the dates along their length and then carefully remove the stones. Chop the ginger into slivers and work them into the marzipan. Place a walnut-size piece of marzipan in the cavity of each date and top with a halved walnut. The dates must be stored in the refrigerator and used within a week.

Right: *Homemade edible gifts are always much appreciated at Christmas.*